VALENTINO ROSSI

Filippo Falsaperla

YAMAHA
YAMAHA
MotoGP
MotoGP
MotoGP
500
250
125

VALENTINO ROSSI

LEGEND

by Filippo Falsaperla

YELLOW JERSEY PRESS
LONDON

CONTENTS

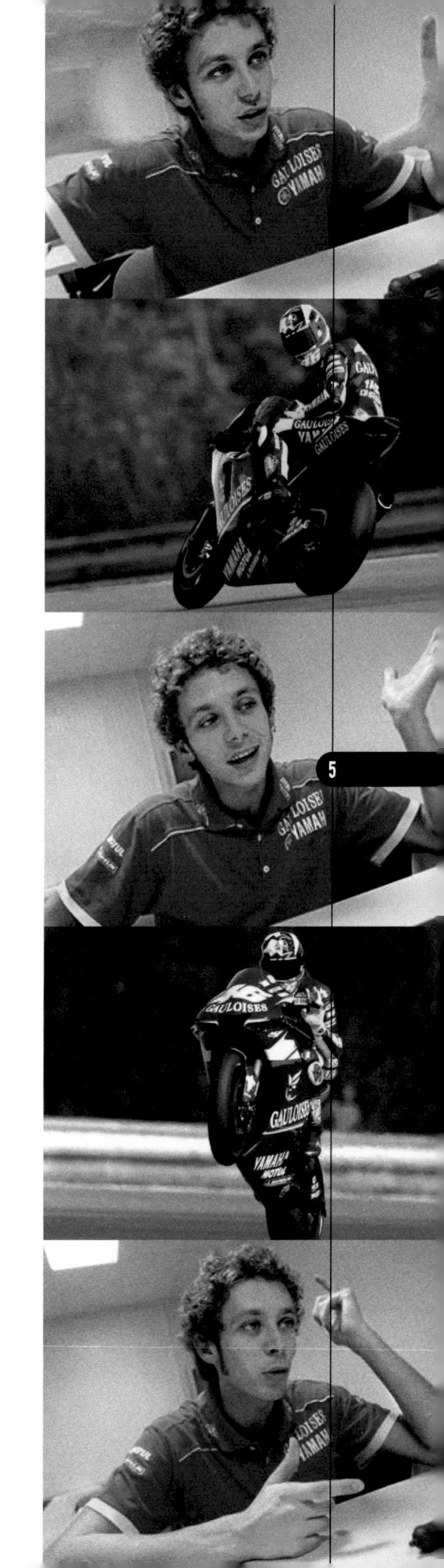

10 YEARS OF **RECORDS** & VICTORIES

It is just a short step from 'Rossifumi' to 'The Doctor'. Ten years of victories, records, impossible overtaking manoeuvres, the odd fall and a whole load of thrills. Along the way there have been disguises, set pieces, witty statements and barbed comments. Welcome to the world of Valentino Rossi, a racing phenomenon in a sport that is much bigger than often perceived. This is a man who has managed to reach out and touch not only the fans who dream of just once taking a bend like he does, but also a wider audience: adoring and smitten young girls, boys who would love to have him as their friend and confidant, women who want to mother the rich, famous and intelligent charmer, and grandmothers who think they know how to tame this tearaway who brings people out in goose pimples with the impossible things he does on a bike.

He has a simple and direct way of dealing both with racing and life that has won over everyday people, celebrities and sport stars alike. Quite simply, he is a global phenomenon. From Mugello to Australia, from the heat and fervour of Spain to the cold restraint of Japan, a sea of yellow moves in his wake on a tidal wave of passion.

Few people could have foreseen this when, on 4 August 1997 in Zeltweg, Austria, riding an Aprilia which even then was cramping his six-foot frame, he won his first 125cc world title not long after turning 17. Just over eight years later, on 25 September 2005 in Sepang, Malaysia, he won his seventh world title in emphatic fashion. He is truly one of a kind: the only rider to have won the world title in four different classes, and with different motorbikes. Nobody else has left Honda, the dominant force in motorcycle racing, to triumph with their sworn enemy Yamaha – and on a much smaller, much less powerful bike in his debut season to boot.

Reared on milk and petrol – only natural for a boy with an ex-rider for a dad and a motorbike fan for a mum – Rossi grew up in the small central Italian town of Tavullia, near Urbino, where, until the invention of the Ape Piaggio (a three-wheeled motorcycle van), the only fun to be had was with scooters. As a kid, he had countless adventures and scrapes, all involving bikes and motors. His first love was karts, but they were too expensive to take beyond the odd local race. Then came a veritable passion for minimoto bikes, ridden to the point of exhaustion round the tracks of the Adriatic Riviera near his home. Later serious racing opportunities would come his way, some perhaps facilitated by his father, though he would fully justify any 'shortcuts' he was offered by succeeding in an extremely difficult, exclusive and financially demanding sport by virtue of his undeniable natural talent.

His career was like that of many others before him, until that fateful 4 August. Perhaps he had it a little easier than others, with an official contract to join the world of the big boys, but Valentino still needed to prove himself in a world where there is more to success than simply beating the stopwatch. He was fast on the track, and a real character off it. He had the spark of theatre just like his dad Graziano, who wore racing clothes consisting of a suit and helmet with fairytale images painted on it, and who drove an old-style globe-like Fiat Multipla. A small guy with a ponytail, Graziano walked around Pesaro one Sunday afternoon with a hen on a lead just to annoy all the 'square' people.

The Valentino phenomenon was born here, from the bar room jokes to the elaborate victory celebrations. He famously celebrated his seventh world title with fans by appearing with Snow White and the Seven Dwarfs, and on another occasion rode a victory lap with a blow-up doll sporting Claudia Schiffer's name – a joke at the expense of his arch-rival Max Biaggi, who had been linked in the papers with Naomi Campbell. The Valentino story encompasses all of this and more, offering thrills, spills and great entertainment. It is a white-knuckle ride through his triumphs and a showcase for all his memorable antics. The story is far from over, however. At 26 Rossi still has a lifetime of dreams ahead, even if the man they call 'The Prodigy' has already won all there is to win.

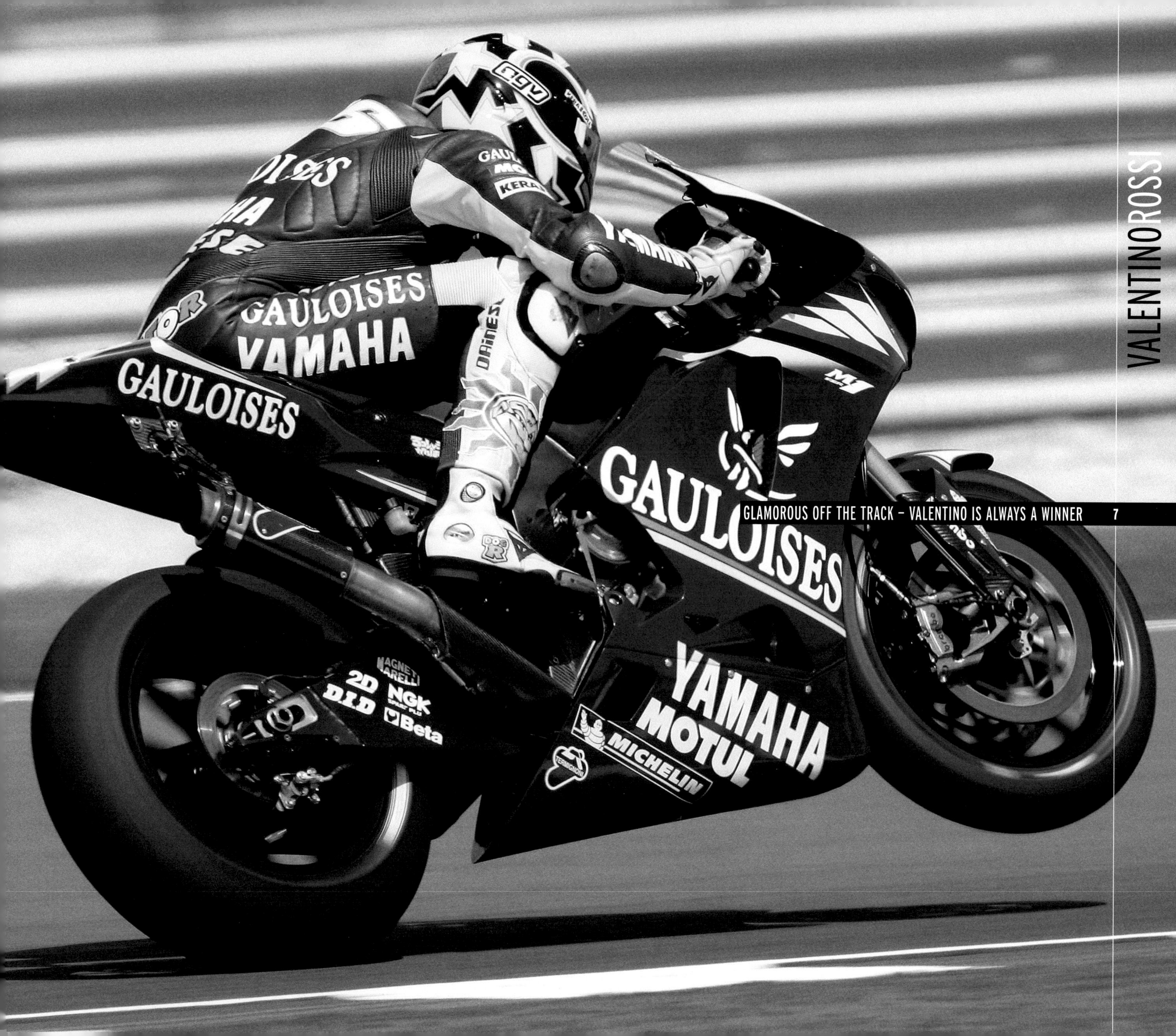

GLAMOROUS OFF THE TRACK – VALENTINO IS ALWAYS A WINNER

THE **PRODIGY** KICKS OFF WITH 11 TRIUMPHS

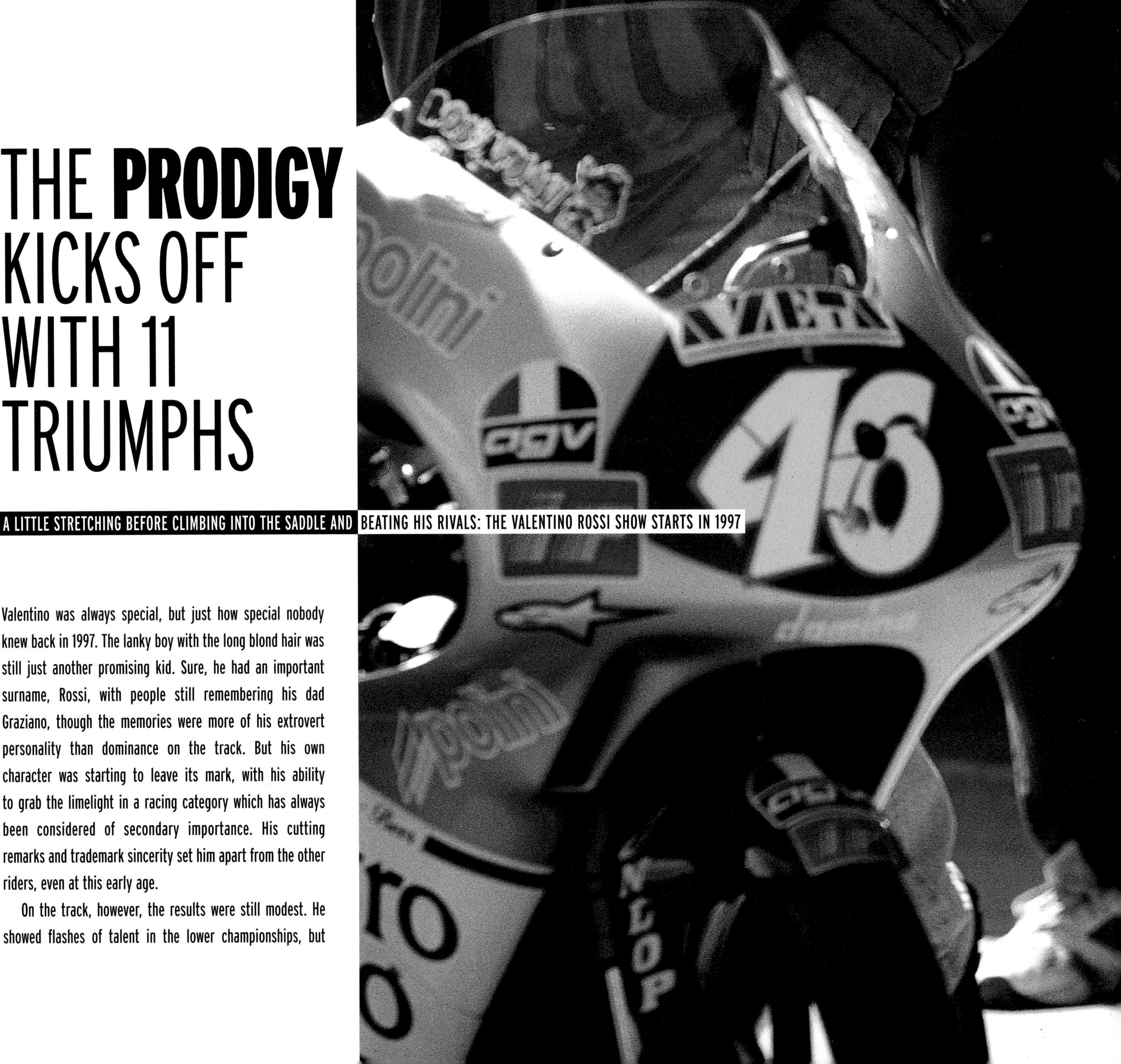

A LITTLE STRETCHING BEFORE CLIMBING INTO THE SADDLE AND BEATING HIS RIVALS: THE VALENTINO ROSSI SHOW STARTS IN 1997

Valentino was always special, but just how special nobody knew back in 1997. The lanky boy with the long blond hair was still just another promising kid. Sure, he had an important surname, Rossi, with people still remembering his dad Graziano, though the memories were more of his extrovert personality than dominance on the track. But his own character was starting to leave its mark, with his ability to grab the limelight in a racing category which has always been considered of secondary importance. His cutting remarks and trademark sincerity set him apart from the other riders, even at this early age.

On the track, however, the results were still modest. He showed flashes of talent in the lower championships, but

I HAVE A THOUSAND RITUALS
ONE GLOVE BEFORE THE OTHER.
I STRETCH, I KNEEL DOWN
BUT I CAN'T REVEAL THEM ALL . . .

A HARD MAN ON THE TRACK, BUT AMIABLE IN EVERYDAY LIFE, VALENTINO ROSSI IS HUGELY POPULAR WITH

THE KIDS, AND HE DRIVES MOTORBIKE RACING FANS CRAZY. THE 18-YEAR-OLD IS UNUSUALLY MATURE AND ALWAYS HAS SOMETHING TO SAY

I HAVE HAPPY MEMORIES OF MY CHILDHOOD AND SOMETIMES I WANT TO BE 7 OR 8 AGAIN, WHEN FUN IS ALL THAT MATTERS

without setting the world alight, despite the excellent bikes he always had. Even his debut in the senior series the year before, with official rider status within his grasp, saw only average performances. In 1996 Valentino won the first race of the season at Brno, showing that he was a good rider. But he still had so much to prove. If anyone, it was another youngster, Ivan Goi, who seemed to be the most prodigious talent, winning at Zeltweg at just 16 years and 157 days, still a record today.

But a single winter can change everything for a 17-year-old boy in the middle of his physical, psychological and, above all, technical development. And that is exactly what happens. Rossi comes of age the following spring and takes 125cc racing by storm. People said it was impossible for someone nearly six foot tall to dominate a 125, a bike specifically designed for a much smaller 'jockey', yet Valentino proves them wrong, stretching his lanky frame over the fuel tank, pushing his bottom out over the tail in order to fully control the little bike.

Rossi also proved it was possible to dominate a class where four ambitious riders were as intent on stopping each other as they were on winning races. But win he did, establishing a record in the class with 11 victories in 15 races. Even then he never failed to entertain, sometimes playing the aloof card, but always fighting until the last bend. The first signs of his refusal to take things seriously can be glimpsed around this time – the jokes, the fooling around – but when the chips are down he slips into a groove, combining utter concentration, maximum effort and precise strategy to enable him always to do the right thing at the right time.

> I TOLD MYSELF 'I WANT TO SEE IF I CAN LOSE THIS RACE'. UNFORTUNATELY, I FOUND A WAY
>
> JAPANESE

HUNCHED BEHIND THE WINDSCREEN, BENT ON REACHING TOP SPEED. VALENTINO IS VERY DEMANDING OF HIS APRILIA 125: THERE IS A WORLD CHAMPIONSHIP TO WIN

Even with a constantly changing set of rivals, he still manages to find the winning moves. Though still lacking in experience, his innate talent shines through, showing why he will soon earn the moniker 'The Prodigy'.

When a display of strength is needed, he goes all out on the attack. In a more tactical race, he plays a waiting game. Valentino gives his all during the season's races, even if it means taking risks. Rossi's risks, however, are always calculated – it is not by chance that his falls are few and far between. It must be said, though, he was not always like this. Take Brazil in 1996. The track there was being used for the first time and an extra day of testing was scheduled. Valentino managed to fall off four times, with team manager Giampiero Sacchi worrying not only about the boy injuring himself, but about all the cost of repairs to the super-expensive carbon fibre bodywork. In that magic year of 1997, the situation changed in a flash. Rossi's motorcycle engineer at the time, Mauro Noccioli, said later that it was simply a technical adjustment, a 'magic' tyre fitted to his bike that allowed him perfect control over the front wheel and thus maximum performance at top speed. His only mistake, a skid at Suzuka, in the den of rivals Honda, proved to be no more than a cameo in the bigger picture.

With his taste for victory keener by the race, Valentino has

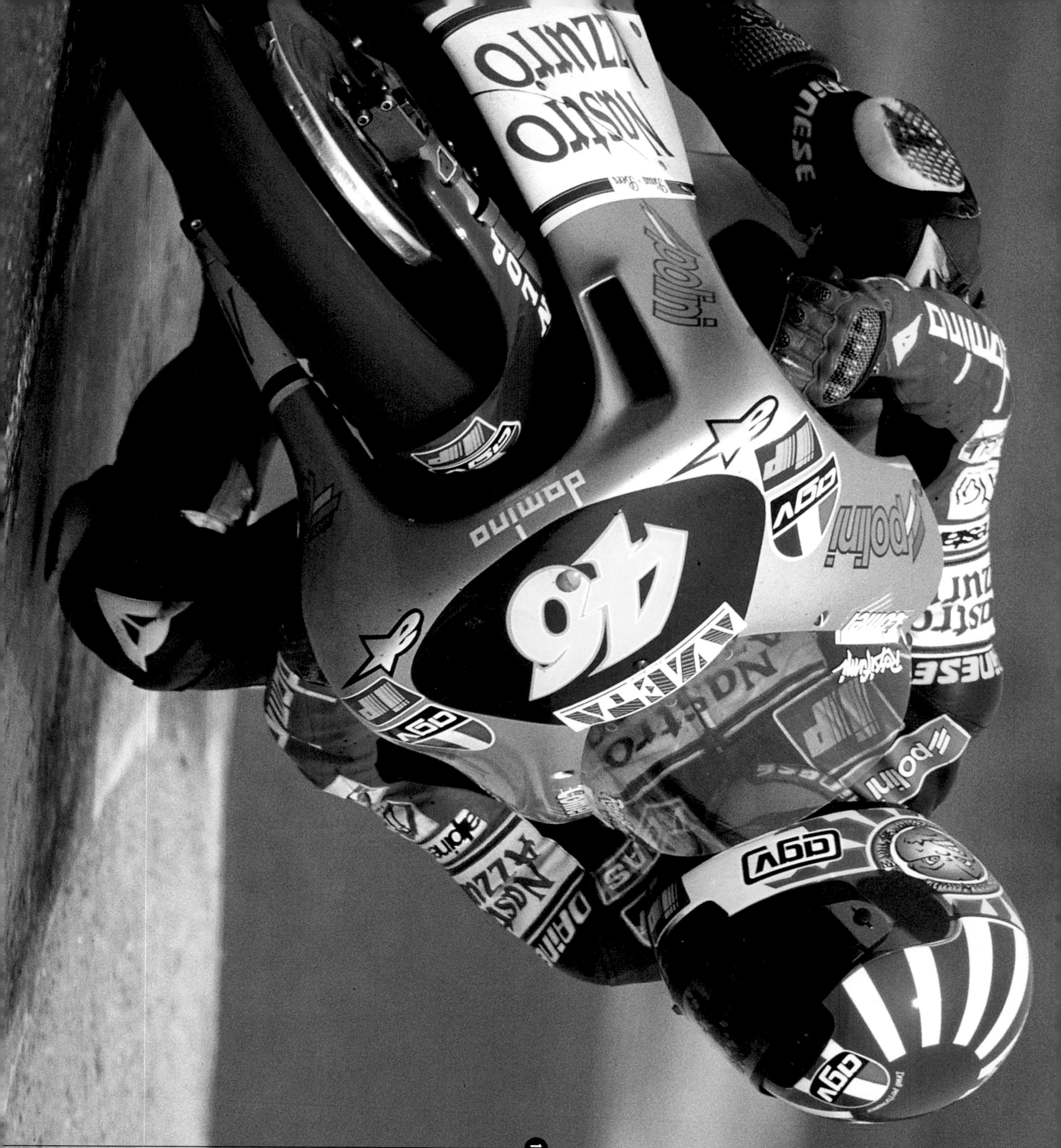
Nastro Azzurro
polini
agv
domino
46

I WAS PLEASED WITH MYSELF WHEN I OVERTOOK UEDA, BUT HE GOT THE BETTER OF ME IN THE END

AUSTRIAN GP

46
polini
domino
polini
Nastro Azzurro
aprilia
agv

I DEDICATE MY WIN TO
WHOEVER THOUGHT UP
THE ANTI-BIAGGI BANNER
IMOLA GP

FOCUSED IN THE PITS, RUTHLESS ON THE TRACK. THIS IS THE HARSH LAW OF VALENTINO ROSSI, THE EMERGING ACE OF THE MOTORCYCLE WORLD CHAMPIONSHIP

no further mishaps that season, stringing together an unbroken series of podium finishes until the last race, in Australia, where he is let down by the bike. 'I can accept that,' he says at the time, 'I made one mistake, the bike is allowed one too.'

Rossi shows no signs of bitterness about it, and the world begins to appreciate this straight-talking and sincere young man. When he pulls off a great win, he can talk about it with remarkable understatement, but when someone deserves praise he rarely needs to be asked twice.

This attitude makes him hugely popular at Noale, home of Aprilia. He is not acting when, in Brazil, he kisses his 'little bike' in gratitude, thanking its super engine for handing him a win. The scene is repeated at Brno after he wraps up the title but, instead of kissing the Aprilia 125, he gets a beautiful girl in a clinch.

He is very respectful of his rivals, both on the track and in interviews with the press. Two key moments that season exemplify this. Kazuto Sakata also rides an Aprilia, although for another team, yet Rossi pays tribute to him with words rarely used by other riders. In Germany, at a rain-soaked Nürburgring, the Japanese rider seems uncatchable until his Aprilia lets him down. 'I only won because Sakata's bike broke,' admits Vale. 'With Ueda and Manako out of the race I only needed second place.'

The second episode mirrors the first, with Sakata's lead ended by Rossi in Barcelona. A spark plug starts playing up, a not infrequent problem with the Aprilia bikes. Kazuto has to slow down and Valentino wins by a long stretch. Later he admits: 'I thought of slowing down and letting him win, but he was too slow and it would have been too obvious.'

polini
Birra · Beer
Nastro Azzurro
Expert Lager
aprilia
BLUE JEANS
GAS
G-SHOCK
CASIO
DUNLOP
MARIANI
adige
DELLORTO
CARBURATORI
DOMINO

BEFORE THE RACE I COULDN'T SAY HELLO TO THE FANS: SORRY, I WAS IN A HURRY

IMOLA GP

IN WHAT IS ALMOST A HOME GP, ROSSI BEATS THE JAPANESE MANAKO WITH A FORMIDABLE DISPLAY OF STRENGTH

20 ROSSI'S LONG LEVERS AND HIS CHARACTERISTIC RIDING STYLE

HE SEEMS TO EMBRACE THE APRILIA 125

He is honest with his rivals, yet ruthless with his 'enemies'. 1997 heralded the start of his long, often aggressive, rivalry with Max Biaggi. The trigger seems to have been an incident before the season's opening Grand Prix in Japan. The story goes that, after a fraught meeting in an Italian restaurant in Suzuka, Max points his finger at the emerging new rider who is taunting him, and says, 'Wash your mouth out before talking about me.' Their enmity becomes an open secret, though Rossi will not have to wait long to avenge the put down. At the next race in Jerez, Spain, Valentino wins and fuels the flames further by remarking: 'A perfect race, but Biaggi not winning in the 250 would make it a perfect day.' And his wish came true. The rivalry between the two riders continues with Rossi winding Biaggi up with the infamous doll incident at Mugello, and planting an irreverent kiss on the Max Biaggi supporters' banner during his lap of honour at Assen.

As a rider, Valentino proves to be much more convincing. His 125's principal shortcoming is that it does not start very well, so his races frequently produce frantic charges, typically in the early stages. This adds zest to a championship which could otherwise have slid into a monotonous series of parades. Valentino wins only a few races by a long stretch, such as the Indonesian GP. Most of them are hard-fought battles, fought on a knife-edge, and sometimes, like in Austria, narrowly lost. This is very much the exception, however, as is to be expected from such a competitive rider.

Valentino shows how battling with an adversary can be used not only as a racing philosophy, but as a stimulus too. Staying in front, out there all on your own, is the easiest way to make a mistake, at least for him. He discovers this at

CLINGING TO THE FENCE LIKE SUPERMAN, MILKING THE FANS' APPLAUSE. MAX BIAGGI'S FANS JOIN THE PARTY. THE TWO ITALIAN MOTORCYC

HERE I'M SIGNING AN AUTOGRAPH EVERY STEP OF THE WAY – AS IT SHOULD BE, IT'S A SPECIAL RACE

IMOLA GP

ALONE AGAINST THE STOPWATCH, WITH HIS RIVALS FALLING FURTHER BEHIND. ROSSI MANAGES TO PUSH THE BOUNDARIES IN 125CC

46
polini
Nastro
Azzurro
aprilia
agv
domino
Birra · Beer
Expert Lager
REGINA
CHAIN
NGK
GAS
BIO
DAINESE
alpinestars

THIS TIME I DON'T DESERVE TO WIN. I FEEL SORRY FOR SAKATA, IF IT WERE NOT FOR THE BREAKDOWN HE WOULD HAVE WON

GERMAN GP

26 ARMS ALOFT, LIKE A CYCLIST WINNING BY A MILE. IT'S A MOMENT OF JOY FOR

THE BOY FROM TAVULLIA. A SCENE WHICH WE WILL GET USED TO SEEING NOT JUST IN 125CC: A STAR IS BORN

Mugello, a race which begins in the worst possible manner. His engine breaks down in the warm-up – a similar incident had happened the year before, only during a race – and the team is forced to change a piston. At the start the bike begins to make a terrible noise, and breaking away from the leading riders seems impossible. But not that Sunday. Alone at the front, Valentino has to seek out an invisible adversary. 'I was scared of falling asleep, so I started pretending I was in a test with lots of things to check so as not to lose my concentration. But after a few laps I got distracted and had to start again from scratch.'

Just another of the tricks of the trade which Rossi was quickly learning. Another was the time in Holland when he cunningly secured victory by using slightly longer than usual gear ratios in order to exploit his rivals' slipstreams in the searingly hot latter stages. But it is in Brazil that we discover Rossi the tactician. It goes without saying that the race is a lengthy duel with Noboru Ueda. While Rossi's Aprilia is much faster than the Honda of the Japanese, the Italian does not want to show his hand. With two laps to go he could easily have overtaken in the straight below the stands. Instead, while Nobby is stuck to the fuel tank of his Honda, squeezing the last few horse power out of his small engine, Rossi lifts himself up off his bike, just enough to stay behind.

But only for one lap, before the decisive all-or-nothing attack that brings another triumph.

Rossi further enhances his burgeoning reputation as a race strategist par excellence later that season at Assen. The Dutch circuit is special, often called the University of Motorcycling,

ROSSIFUMI
polini
agv
158

MY NICKNAME?
WHEN I SAW NORIFUMI'S DISPLAY,
I BECAME ROSSIFUMI

and it is there that the greats stand out. Valentino is riding it like he has an extra gear, but then he makes a mistake. His left hand goes for the throttle, while with his right he tries to adjust the brake lever for the front wheel. The move is quick, but it costs him several places. Despite that, Valentino recovers, and puts on a fantastic comeback with a memorable last lap. His team insist afterwards that it was just an excuse to put on a bit of a show! Rossi's dad Graziano also won on this track, riding a Morbidelli 250 in 1979, marking a father-son double that had only been done once before, by Nello and Alberto Pagani. Valentino gives further evidence that season that when seriousness is required, he can focus fully on the objective. Take the race at Brno, the track where he was crowned champion. With four races to go and the title within his grasp, Rossi had time on his side. But the race in the Czech Republic seems to be the perfect stage for his coronation, and Vale is determined to take the crown at the first time of asking. Half of Tavullia have made the trip to celebrate with their hero, but then the sun comes out after two days of rain, causing problems for the whole field of riders. The set-ups are only decided on at the last minute during the warm-up, and for once Valentino does not look too comfortable. His main rival, Ueda, seems determined to give him a hand, however, starting off well back in 18th position. But the Japanese rider has no desire to stay there and soon takes control of the race. Rossi, holding onto fourth place, knows that only a podium finish will seal the title and is in no mood to postpone the party.

A little good fortune (in the form of a penalty for the leader after some not atypical 125cc chaos), combined with a couple of breathtaking surges brings Valentino the third place

VALENTINO IN CONTROL IN THE MIDDLE OF THE PACK. A CAUTIOUS APPROACH FOR ONCE. BRNO IS THE RACE

THAT CAN GIVE HIM THE TITLE: HE HAS TO USE HIS HEAD

THE WORLD CHAMPIONSHIP IS TOO IMPORTANT:
I ONLY THOUGHT ABOUT THE TITLE

CZECH REPUBLIC GP

46
agv
Ringo
ROSSIFUMI
Comel
polini
aprilia
dainese
alpinestars
Comel
domino

'WHETHER YOU LIKE IT OR NOT, YOUR MOTORHOME BECOMES YOUR HOME FOR SIX MONTHS OF THE YEAR. DURING THE GRANDS PRIX YOU CAN HIDE

I LOVE YELLOW BECAUSE IT IS HAPPINESS AND THE COLOUR OF ENERGY AND OF THE SUN. AND IT MAKES MY BIKE STAND OUT FROM THE FIELD

FROM THE WORLD AND FIND YOUR FOCUS. MY FRIEND UCCIO USUALLY DRIVES IT: MINE HAS EVERY IMAGINABLE HOME COMFORT, INCLUDING A PLAYSTATION'

36 PERFECT SHAPE FOR A DEMANDING BEND: VALENTINO MAKES

I HARDLY SLEPT, AT 1AM
I WAS ALREADY AWAKE, SO I
WENT TO HAVE A HAMBURGER.
THEN I WATCHED F1 ON TV,
BUT AT 7 I WAS READY

INDONESIAN GP

EVEN THE HARDEST TRACKS LOOK EASY WITH HIS PRECISE TRAJECTORIES

VALENTINO QUICKLY BECOMES A PHENOMENON, POPULAR WITH THE FANS, A PERSONALITY ON

I HAVE TO DO ADVERTS, GO TO GALA EVENTS AND DINNERS. I DON'T LIKE IT BUT IT'S BETTER THAN GETTING UP EACH MORNING TO GO TO WORK IN A FACTORY

THE TRACK WHO ALSO MANAGES TO BE A STAR IN FRONT OF THE CAMERAS: IT'S ONE OF THE QUALITIES OF CHAMPIONS

I RELAX WITH SPEED. I HAVE WAYS TO MAKE SURE I GIVE IT MY ALL

agv
DAINESE
Nastro
polini
domino
agv
polini

I'LL NEVER FORGET MY FIRST WORLD TITLE

WITH DAD GRAZIANO ON THE PODIUM AT BRNO

he needs. In his own way, the champion shows how much that result means to him. He did what was asked of him and has been rewarded with a much-deserved world title. It is just the first of many key moments in which Valentino will turn difficulty into triumph.

Rossi then wanted to put his seal on the season with an emphatic finish. After winning the race at Sentul in Indonesia, the penultimate event of the season, he declares: 'I want to win the next race in Australia to end my 125cc adventure on a high.' However, a brief cylinder misfire while he is fighting for the lead puts paid to his dream and he finishes a disappointing fourth. Nonetheless, the imminent prospect of switching to an Aprilia 250 is a nice consolation. The adventure has only just begun.

CHASING, CATCHING AND **BREAKING AWAY**

VALENTINO POWERS OFF WITH THE DISTINCTIVE NUMBER 46. NUMBER 1 IS FOR REIGNING CHAMPION CAPIROSSI: IT IS A DUEL WHICH SETS THE 250 CLASS ALIGHT

A great many people assumed Rossi would cruise to the title in 1999, but this was far from the case. What should have been a triumphant parade turned into a hard-fought affair, with victory only secured in the penultimate race. Billed as the champion-in-waiting when he makes his debut in the 250cc class in 1998, his first season does not go quite as planned and he finishes second, 23 points behind the champion. This is still good for a rookie who has been pitted against veterans such as Loris Capirossi and Tetsuya Harada, all riding the same, invincible Aprilia. In a season dominated by Aprilia, Valentino nonetheless picks up five race wins in his new class – but perhaps more importantly bucketloads of invaluable experience.

GIVI
GIVI
21
34
46
Nastro Azzurro
4
ADVANCE
elf
elf
HONDA

I DON'T KNOW WHAT HAPPENED, THE GEARS DIDN'T WORK, NEITHER DID THE ENGINE. A DISASTER

MALAYSIAN GP

The Japanese teams, for different reasons, came into the 1999 season in difficulty – Honda due to an apparent lack of interest, and Yamaha because of the limitations of its 250cc bike. In addition, the list of title contenders was shortened considerably. The Japanese rider Harada was persuaded by Aprilia to take the plunge into the treacherous waters of two-cylinder 500cc racing. World champion Capirossi, meanwhile, who was dropped abruptly by Aprilia after an alleged incident in the decisive race in Argentina involving a Japanese team-mate, managed to obtain a wild card place with Honda, practically foregoing a signing-on fee to join Fausto Gresini's team.

What should have been a triumphant parade thus becomes a thrilling season. In the end, it is fought harder than the greatest optimist could have expected, although it does give the world of motorcycling perhaps the best Valentino Rossi performance of his career. Subsequent 500cc and MotoGP titles will be undoubtedly epic achievements, but in 1999 Valentino finds the perfect compromise between a sporting maturity that sees him post an incredible 9 wins in 16 races, a ratio that will set him on the way to becoming the highest-scoring rider of all time, and an off-track intelligence.

Though no longer a boy – he has by then enough experience to deal with life in the spotlight – Rossi still possesses the youthful spontaneity that gave rise to many of his legendary antics.

The odd frustration at being misinterpreted by the press will later cause Rossi to go on the defensive, carefully picking his words and maintaining a line of 'political correctness'. But not back then. Every race becomes a show, with ever more

DAD GRAZIANO WATCHES HIS SON, WHILE VALENTINO LOOKS TO THE HORIZON.

I SHOWED EVERYONE. I AM REALLY ENJOYING THIS BECAUSE IT ONLY TAKES TWO RACES FOR PEOPLE TO START QUESTIONING YOU

SPANISH GP

THE 250CC WORLD CHAMPIONSHIP TURNS OUT TO BE A SCRAMBLE FOR THE TITLE: CAPIROSSI AND UKAWA START STRONG, BUT ROSSI IS WAITING

*THE BIKE IS EXTREMELY FAST ON THE STRAIGHT.
I MAKE THE DIFFERENCE ON THE BIG BENDS*

LEANING IN WITH TYPICAL DETERMINATION. AT EVERY BEND VALENTINO ROSSI PUSHES HIS APRILIA TO THE LIMIT: THE WORLD CHAMPIONSHIP IS PLAYED OUT ON A KNIFE EDGE

THE HARDEST WAY TO WIN? BREAKING AWAY AND NEVER BEING CAUGHT

I WAS SO EXCITED AS A CHILD WHEN I TOUCHED THE GROUND WITH MY KNEE FOR THE FIRST TIME WHILE RIDING A MOTORBIKE

MASTER OF HIS MOTORBIKE, AND OF THE TRACK

'CAPIROSSI OUT' THEY SAID FROM THE PITS. THEN I SAW THE BLACK FLAG WITH THE NUMBER 1. IT WASN'T MINE, SO I CALMED DOWN

ITALIAN GP

RIVALS ON THE TRACK, FRIENDS OFF IT. LORIS CAPIROSSI AND VALENTINO

ROSSI KNOW HOW TO RELIEVE THE TENSION, EVEN IF IN RACES THEY GO AT IT HAMMER AND TONGS. IT ENDS IN WORLD CHAMPIONSHIP JOY

elaborate disguises, as he proves himself to be both unpredictable and unmissable.

He is harsh and cutting in his criticism of others, but judges himself by the same standards. After his daring victory at Mugello, ruined by a spectator track invasion that prevented him from acting out a set-piece he had prepared with his fan-club friends – he even falls off his bike in the ensuing chaos after colliding with photographer Gigi Soldano – he says harshly: 'I must thank my chief engineer Rossano Brazzi because he looked at all the data and drew his own conclusions. He told me I'd got it all wrong. Perhaps he was right, but we have to come to an agreement with the other riders. They're going to have to go slower in practice or faster in the race . . .' There is also a bout of self-criticism at Imola where, after being well on his way to winning the title, he is soundly beaten by Capirossi. 'He (Capirossi) had nothing to lose, while I succumbed to nerves. I started thinking about the world title, about my mum. I lost my concentration, making it even harder not to mess up.'

As quick as he is to criticise himself and his team, he can also be fulsome in his praise. After the key victory in South Africa, the champion refuses to take all the credit, saying: 'The bike is extremely fast on the straights, I just make the difference on the big bends.'

The flip side is in evidence at Brno when, after beating German team-mate Ralf Waldmann, he remarks: 'Luckily Witteveen promised me the German would help me . . .' He also criticises the Noale company, not their engineers, of course, but those in charge of sponsorship, when a placard is displayed in Argentina hailing victory in the constructors'

agv
VALENTINIK
DIESEL
VALENTINIK
DIESEL
aprilia
aprilia
Nastro Azzurro
BREIL
PlayStation
aprilia
aprilia
Nastro

A BEE GOT INTO MY HELMET BUT I JUST LIFTED THE VISOR AND IT FLEW OFF WITHOUT HURTING ME

CATALAN GP

VALENTINO ALWAYS PUTS ON A SHOW, EVEN WHEN HE'S UPSTAGED BY THE BIG WHEEL

UKAWA GOT LUCKY FOR HALF A SEASON, THIS TIME HE PAID FOR HIS MISTAKES

GERMAN GP

VALENTINO ROSSI WINS A LONG DUEL WITH CAPIROSSI AT THE SACHSENRING. IT IS A KEY WIN AS UKAWA COMES OFF AND SCORES NO POINTS. AT MID POINT IN THE SEASON ROSSI LEADS THE 250CC CLASS

championship. 'When I won my title they didn't do anything, and now they bring out this placard. They have no style. If I'd seen it before the finish, I would have stopped,' the Italian rails.

The controversy with Capirossi in South Africa is even harsher, prompting Rossi to berate his rival: 'After testing he [Capirossi] said that when Honda is on form it can beat anyone, and that he'd won pole with his race tyres. How can he talk like that? He's been kicked in the teeth for nearly the whole season but he still comes out with these things. It's just given me another reason to win, not that I needed one.'

Rossi is oozing determination, and the duel with Capirossi adds even more spice than usual to the 250cc world championship just as the season approaches the midway point and its summer break. However, Capirossi then had a series of poor races, and Rossi begins to think about a move to the 500cc class the following season. Nonetheless, theirs was a classic rivalry, amplified by a degree of animosity and, not least, by the fact that they are both Italians. It is an explosive mix which finds the ideal fuse in Assen midway through the season, and will reach boiling point in a breathtaking head-to-head in Germany.

Coming into the Assen event, Loris is determined to make up lost ground after picking up a two-race suspension for hitting Lucchi at Mugello. By contrast, Valentino seems to be lacking the hunger for victory that often allows him to win races at the last possible moment. In any event, victory goes to Loris, with Rossi berating himself and later saying: 'I looked a real turnip losing that race.' Just one week later, however, Valentino enjoys the sweetest of revenges in the rain

VALENTINO CONTINUES HIS MARCH OF GLORY WITH APRILIA RIDING A 250

I AM NEVER HAPPY
WITH SECOND PLACE,
I ONLY WANT TO WIN

AFTER DOMINATING THE 125CC WORLD CHAMPIONSHIP IN 1997

THE MAN FROM TAVULLIA MAKES IT A FANTASTIC DOUBLE

at Donington, beating Capirossi on the track where his rival has won four world championship races, including his first ever and a famous win in the European Grand Prix. Rossi is on cloud nine after his win and ends the race with typical antics, including kisses for his Aprilia and the proclamation: 'I wanted to come back strongly after losing in Holland. If only all races were like this.' Back-to-back wins are secured with victory at Sachsenring in Germany, where the race is once again between the two fantastic Italians. Riding bike to bike, with little overtaking due to the narrow track but bags of tension nonetheless, Capirossi breaks away and leads for a while, only for Valentino to hit the front and dictate proceedings. Loris then tries to muscle back into the lead in the closing stages, but he fails and finishes in Valentino's slipstream. Victory gives Rossi the lead in the championship, a position he will defend until the end of the season. After bad luck in the first two races of the season and a win to put him back on track, Vale prepares to pile on the suffering for his rival at the French GP, where there is to be another twist in the tale.

In France he dominates the race from the start, focusing solely on celebrating another victory. But with half a lap to go, his chain inexplicably comes off. It is almost an impossibility, though it has also happened to Marcellino Lucchi in testing and to Franco Battaini in a race, both with Aprilia. Some 25 deserved and precious points thus slip from his grasp to be gratefully picked up by Tohru Ukawa, who will go on to become Rossi's main rival for the rest of the season. Later, after he had won the title, Valentino explains the unlucky episode with a semi-mystical 'parable'. 'In all this year's races, my guardian angel (i.e. Flavio Fratesi, the "angel" of

'(ANOTHER OF MY NICKNAMES) "VALENTINIK" WAS CREATED ON HOLIDAY IN TUNISIA IN 1998. I CHOSE HIM BECAUSE HE'S NOT

INVINCIBLE LIKE SUPERMAN – THOUGH HE IS VERY LIKEABLE.' IT BECOMES VALE'S MONIKER IN 250 RACING

WALDMANN WAS IN THE LEAD FOR THE FIRST TIME BUT IF HE'D WON HE WOULD HAVE GOT TOO EXCITED. THIS WAY HE'LL STAY CALM

CZECH REPUBLIC GP

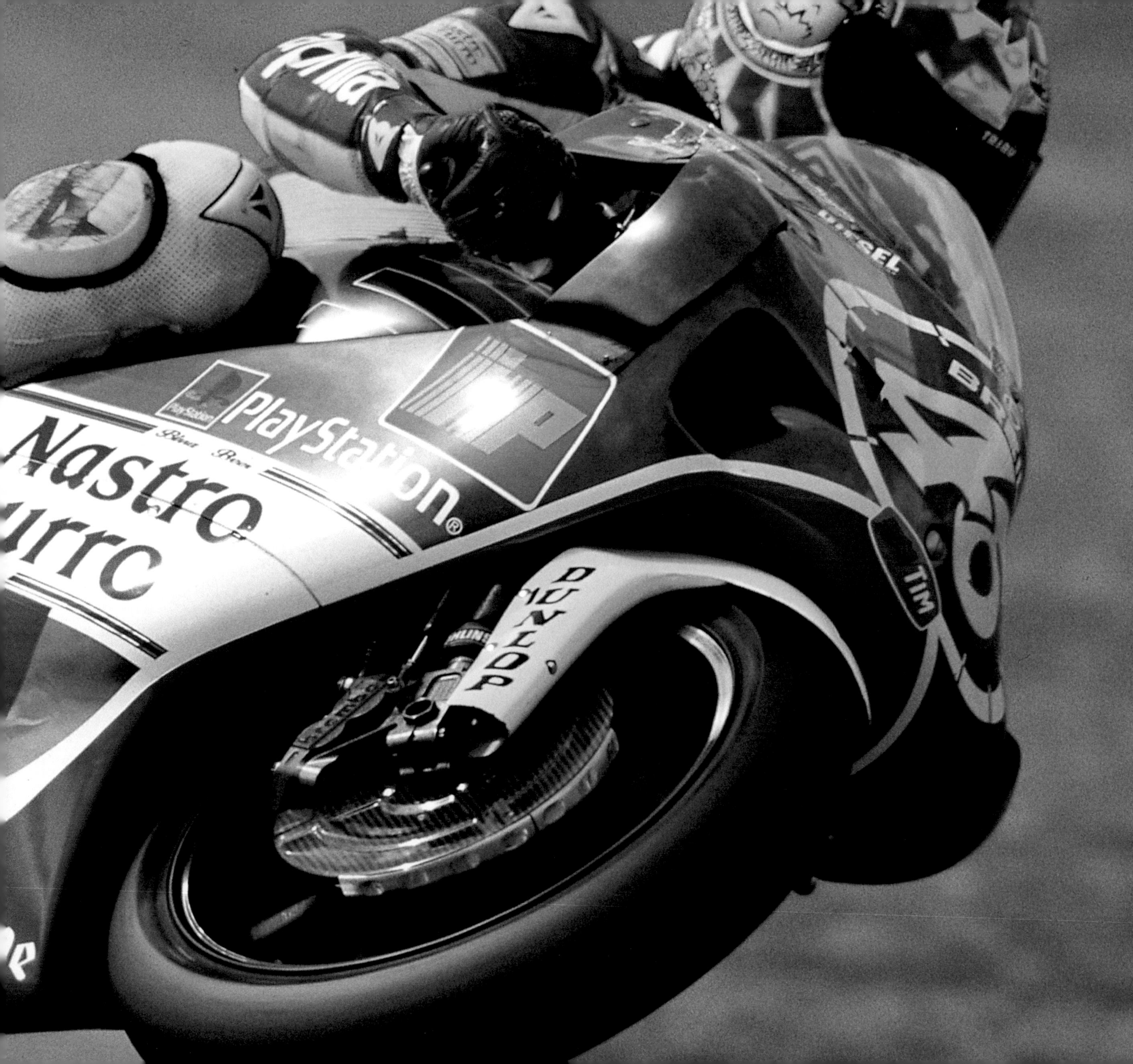
Nastro
PlayStation
DUNLOP
TIM

FOCUSED AT THE START WITH THE PIT LANE GIRL.

I CAN CONTROL THE BIKE, TACTICS, EVERYTHING: I WASN'T LIKE THIS A YEAR AGO

OSSI IS READY FOR ANOTHER SHOW

VALENTINO ROSSI LEADS THE FIELD, FOLLOWED BY UKAWA (4), CAPIROSSI (1) AND PERUGINI (7). HE WINS 9 RACES IN 1999

I COULD HAVE BEEN STRATEGIC, BUT I WENT ALL OUT TO TEACH CAPIROSSI A LESSON

SOUTH AFRICAN GP

I DON'T LIKE RAIN, I HATE IT.
BUT I'M GETTING USED TO IT

the lap of honour in Brazil) was there. However, he couldn't make it to France.' Perhaps this was the reason, or maybe it was just bad luck (the edges of the Castellet circuit made the back end of the Aprilia bump too hard), but it's a defeat. As a result Rossi has to chase Ukawa hard.

He manages this in the ninth race of the season, in Germany, and races impeccably for the rest of the championship. In the Czech Republic, after the summer break, he puts on a great attacking performance, before carrying out a damage limitation exercise at Imola. He then defends tooth and nail in the wet in Valencia after risking a collision with Olivier Jacque on the second bend, almost withdrawing because his bike was playing up (the Aprilia being no fan of the rain either). After this, Rossi's season builds to a climax. In Australia he secures a pivotal win on the last lap, beating the Frenchman again – a feat Vale will later describe as 'the best lap of my career'. In South Africa, Valentino comes up just short in his bid to seal the title, taking the season down to its final two races in South America.

At the start of the penultimate race in Rio de Janeiro, Rossi needs only three points to be sure of the title. Unused to being in that position, the youngster admits later that he was overcome by nerves at the start (like at Imola) and could not prevent himself being sucked back into the field. At the end of the first lap he is back in 12th place, four-and-a-half seconds off the lead. He finds himself battling against riders with nothing to lose and seemingly no other motivation than to put a spanner in his works. 'You can't do what Criville [the 500cc champion] did and seal a championship without a podium finish,' he will say later. So Rossi throws caution to the

VALENTINO WINS IN RIO AND WINS HIS SECOND TITLE. HIS MECHANICS GO CRAZY AT THE PIT WALL. THE PARTY BEGINS FOR THE PESARO MAN AND

HE TEAM FROM NOALE. ONE THING IS CERTAIN: A LEGEND IS BORN

Marlboro
Marlboro
REPSOL
VÍA
DIGITAL
HONDA
MoviStar
axo
VICEROY
Vía Digital
DUNLOP
Nastro Azzurro
aprilia
agv
SONY
DIESEL
PlayStation
Nastro Azzurro
DUNLOP
Fortuna
REPSOL
HONDA
REPSOL

LASSIC GROUP PICTURE [LEFT] OF THE THREE WORLD CHAMPIONS OF 1999. ROSSI [CENTRE] IS BETWEEN THE TWO SPANIARDS, EMILIO ALZAMORA [125CC CHAMPION] AND ALEX CRIVILLE [WINNER OF THE 500CC]

wind and starts reeling in the leaders. And after eight laps, at 16.00 GMT, he takes the lead. Ukawa, Capirossi and Jacque are hot on his heels, intent on spoiling his party, but nothing can stop him that day. Asked to explain his second world championship title, Valentino later says: 'It was because my Guardian Angel was there for me. We only managed to find 19 plane tickets for the 20 fan club friends, but somehow he made it.'

Rossi achieved victory with focus and determination on the track, and plenty of fun and imagination off it. For the celebrations he dons a special t-shirt, bearing the words 'Two-times World Champion' in comically misspelled Italian, and thanks his legions of fans. This is more or less how his adventure in 250cc ends. Just like in 1997, he is unable to salute his fans with a win in the final race in Argentina, as he would like, after tyre problems see him finish behind Jacque and Ukawa. However, he soon gets over the disappointment. It is not yet official, but everything is in place for his move up to 500cc, where he can aspire to repeating Phil Read and Mike Hailwood's feat of winning world titles in three different categories. Aprilia tries desperately to keep him, offering him huge amounts of money, but the allure of the official Honda NSR 500 is too much. Mick Doohan's bike, the bike of dreams, beckons, and Rossi will not be sidetracked.

VALENTINO WEARING APRILIA RACING COLOURS AND AN UNUSUAL HAT. IT IS HIS LAST SEASON WITH THE NOALE TEAM BEFORE HIS MOVE TO HONDA, BUT HIS ANTICS WILL CONTINUE WITH THE JAPANESE OUTFIT

CONTROVERSY WITH APRILIA. IN ARGENTINA, ROSSI IS ANGERED BY A LARGE PLACARD CELEBRATING THE CONSTRUCTORS

YOU'LL SOON KNOW WHO I'LL BE RACING WITH IN 2000. I CAN TELL YOU THAT I WON'T RACE IN BOTH 250 AND 500, BUT JUST ONE OF THEM

ARGENTINIAN GP

CHAMPIONSHIP WIN. 'IF I'D SEEN IT I'D HAVE STOPPED. THERE WAS NO SUCH PLACARD FOR ME WINNING THE TITLE IN RIO'

A **DREAM** HAT-TRICK 125CC, 250CC, **500CC**

 VALENTINO AND THE HONDA NSR: A PERFECT MATCH TO CLOSE OUT THE 500 ERA IN STYLE. FOUR-STROKES APPEAR IN 2002

Valentino Rossi's dream comes true with his best win, sealing a hat-trick of titles won every other year between 1997 and 2001. A year of apprenticeship and then the title – it was like that in 1997 with the 125cc, in 1999 with the 250cc, and then in 2001 with the 500cc. There is great disappointment in 2000 when Rossi throws away a chance to win on his debut in the senior series. He finishes second, 39 points behind Kenny Roberts Jnr, a champion he could have beaten if only he had been quicker in gaining the self-confidence he had by mid-season. 'I started off as if I'd already been beaten: a mistake I'll never make again,' he said ruefully as the title slipped from his grasp.

He takes to 500cc very quickly, or to the Honda 500 to be

46
DEI CHIHUAHUA
MICHELIN
agv
THE DOCTOR
HONDA
Nastro
BREIL
WATCHES
HONDA

BIAGGI IS ALWAYS DIFFICULT TO OVERTAKE. WHEN HE SEES YOU ALONGSIDE HE LETS GO OF THE BRAKES AND CUTS IN

JAPANESE GP

precise. The Aprilia school, with its temperamental bike and great engineers, gave him a breadth of knowledge that allows him to show all his natural talent when he switches to that perfect racing machine, the NSR. His chief engineer, Jeremy Burgess, one of the best around, takes less than a day to realise the talent that Rossi has to offer. The dyed-in-the-wool Australian is immediately awestruck by the Italian thunderbolt, 'betraying' his great countryman Mick Doohan by saying: 'You get the chance to work with a talent like this once in a lifetime. And only if you're lucky.' Together they laid the foundations during an excellent 2000 and swept the board completely in 2001. That season's triumphant procession, which sees Rossi open up a 100-point lead, puts his name in the record books alongside legends such as Giacomo Agostini (11 wins in a season), Phil Read and Mike 'The Bike' Hailwood, the only riders to have won the title in three different classes. Perhaps most importantly of all, however, he brings the senior class title back to Italy 19 years after the world title triumph of Franco Uncini, a rider who, together with Marco Lucchinelli and Virginio Ferrari, lit up an extraordinary era for Italian motorcycling. By 2001, the sport is again very much an Italian affair, with Max Biaggi and Loris Capirossi flanking Rossi on the podiums. That 2000 season has a bit of everything, from extraordinary breakaways to victories decided by hundredths of seconds, from compliments to heated arguments.

The best, however, is still to come.

Valentino lavishes praise on his (sometimes) friend Loris, while all the time keeping up the war of words with Max. After years of verbal sparring, wind-ups and jokes, the two now

BIAGGI, CAPIROSSI AND I RAISED THE LEVEL OF 500 RACING CONSIDERABLY

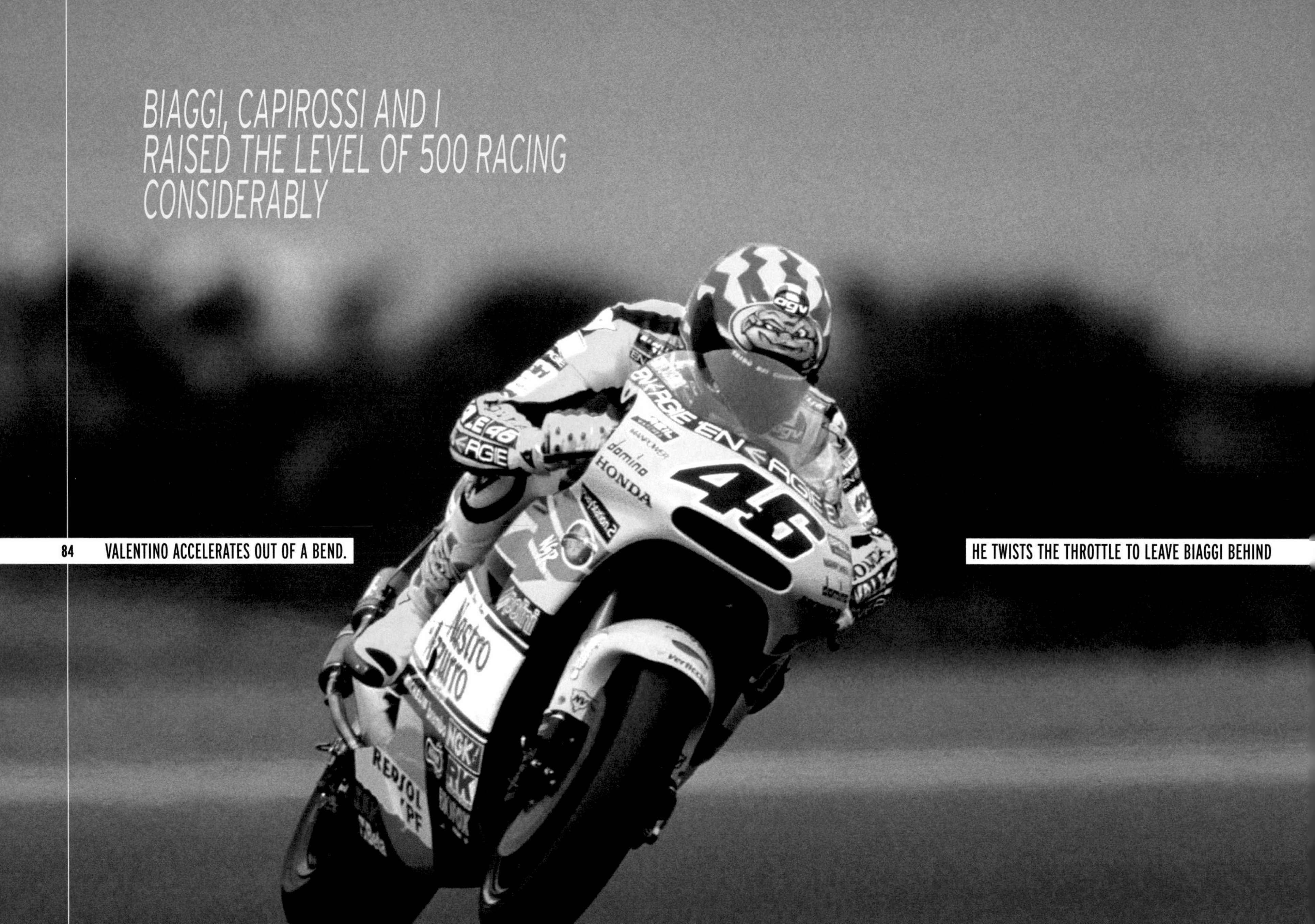

 VALENTINO ACCELERATES OUT OF A BEND. HE TWISTS THE THROTTLE TO LEAVE BIAGGI BEHIND

agv
'ENERGIE 'EN
46
BREIL
MANPOWER
domino
HONDA
HONDA
PlayStation
Nastro Azzurro
3
Marlboro
Marlboro
YAMAHA

I NEVER LOOKED BACK,
I JUST PUSHED AND PUSHED
TO LEAVE BIAGGI BEHIND

JAPANESE GP

finally find themselves racing on the same track, and heated exchanges are inevitable. They both recognise each other's riding talent, but their different personalities, behaviour and lifestyle frequently see sparks fly. The year 2000 is relatively calm as the two riders size each other up on the track, but 2001 sees them lock horns in spectacular fashion in a battle for supremacy.

The tone is set at Suzuka, Japan, in the first race of the year. With the group still bunched together on the fifth lap, Biaggi surges out (in fifth position) and throttles it. 500cc bikes are powerful beasts and it takes just a few gear changes to reach 200kmh. The track is not very wide, but Valentino, who has a better line on the way out of the bend, overtakes on the outside. Or rather he tries to, as Max pushes out, lifts his elbow a little to defend his position and forces Rossi onto the narrow strip of grass. It is a very dangerous move, and one that will not be forgotten. Half a lap later and Rossi attacks Biaggi on the 180-degree 'spoon' bend. Again, they almost make contact, but this time nothing happens. At the end of the main straight, Valentino slips past his rival in a brilliant move and, while still at full tilt in the bend, gives him the finger.

'It was not a polite gesture,' Rossi admits after the race, 'but it was certainly less dangerous than what he did.' The fuse had been lit and sparks fly in the press conference with Valentino warning ominously: 'If this is how it's going to be, then I'm ready for anything. But it might be better not to take it too far.' Lessons are learned – there are no repeat incidents on the track, but what happens off it is a different matter altogether.

In Barcelona, motorcycle fans celebrate one of three

LIKE IN 1999, LORIS AND VALE FIGHT FOR THE TITLE, BUT THIS TIME THE

I BEAT A LORIS IN GREAT FORM. I DIDN'T BREAK AWAY, HALF A SECOND WAS ENOUGH

SOUTH AFRICAN GP

46
domino
HONDA
Nastro
Azzurro
REPSOL
YPF

46
MANPOWER
domino
HONDA
agv

RIDING A HONDA IS A TRIUMPH. YOU EITHER NEED TO BE JAPANESE OR REALLY GOOD

 ROSSI TAKES THE HONDA NSR'S 190 BHP ROUND THE TRACK. HIS UNMISTAKEABLE STYLE AND THE CURVES OF THE BIKE ARE A SHOW WITHIN A SHOW. BARROS (NUMBER 4) IS AN ACE UP HONDA'S SLEEVE TOO

all-Italian podium finishes of the season. The race is a thriller – Valentino starts badly, but takes just a few laps to catch up. From there he goes on to battle it out with Biaggi and Capirossi, eventually leaving them in his wake to win the race and delight his fans. Afterwards the scenes are chaotic in the interview area, which leads via a small spiral staircase to the podium balcony. There are too many people – friends, managers, press and hangers-on – squashed together in a small space. Someone is accidentally hit and insults start flying. Just as in a street brawl it is impossible to say who starts it, who (if anyone) is in the right, and who does the hitting. Valentino ends up with a scratched eyebrow, Max with a black eye. The podium celebrations are about to be cancelled when constructors Honda and Yamaha issue a joint statement calling for calm, and diplomacy prevails.

The after-race protocol changes after that, with strict limitations on access to the enclosure. In the next race, at Assen, the two riders shake hands and, from then on, their rivalry is played out in a sportsmanlike fashion. This all-Italian contest makes for gripping viewing when Valentino and Max go head-to-head at Mugello. The rain pours down on the riders and stoic crowd, who deserve medals for the way they stand firm in the mud bath along the track, and then queue for hours to go home in the logjam of little roads around the

I LIKE THE CUT AND THRUST, I DON'T LIKE NARROW TRACKS, WHERE IT'S HARD TO MAKE A DIFFERENCE

THE CHAMPIONSHIP?
IT'S OVER!

SPANISH GP (THIRD RACE)

Nastro Azzurro
agv
46
ENERGIE
HONDA
domino
Nastro Azzurro
NGK
RK
REPSOL YPF

agv
46
TRIBÙ DEI CHIHUAHUA
agv
HONDA
HONDA RACING
REPSOL YPF

WHEN I WON HERE,
THE TITLE FOLLOWED

SPANISH GP

HONDA
BREIL
MANPOWER
'EN RGIE
46
agv
HONDA

ON THIS BIKE I'M FAST IN THE WET TOO

ITALIAN GP

Tuscan circuit. It could and perhaps should have been Valentino's party, but instead of victory under blue skies as he had hoped, he ended up drowning in the rain with the added disappointment of failing to win the much-hyped race. By the time the race gets underway after a long rain delay, tensions are running especially high. Rossi lines up in pole position, gets a poor start and has just made up the lost ground when the rain comes down again. The race is restarted but in the warm-up lap Rossi somehow takes a spill despite going no faster than his 'grandma driving to the shops'. Disappointed, he goes back to the pits on his friend Gianni Rolando's scooter. The spare bike is waiting on the starting grid and, after a brief delay to allow the star rider to get ready, they tear off. With Rossi's adrenaline levels by then sky high, he almost pulls off an amazing recovery, before fate contrives to deny him.

It is almost a perfect race, but with victory just a few hundred metres away a white line hidden by a puddle ruins his dream. It is pure bad luck, and Alex Barros wins ahead of Capirossi and Biaggi – an outcome all the more surprising given that, over the course of the entire season, there are only two races not won by Valentino or Max: this one at Mugello, and the one in Valencia, where Gibernau posts a memorable win.

That aside, Valentino's championship performances are electrifying. First in Japan, when he gives Honda victory number 500, then in South Africa when he has a wonderful battle with Capirossi, who was forced off the track at the first bend by Roberts. He is first again at Jerez, after a tactical race, in which, ironically, he finds himself up against his boyhood idol Norifumi Abe (who inspired his first nickname). He

LAST YEAR I FELL 1.5 KMS FROM THE FINISH LINE, THIS TIME IT WAS 300 METRES. NEXT YEAR I'LL WIN

ITALIAN GP

easily powers past Abe to open up a seemingly unassailable lead in the world championship. But then comes the defeat, if that is what we can call it, in France, with two Yamahas in front and, worst of all, his nemesis Biaggi winning. Rossi's Honda plays up inexplicably when crossing the finish line – suspected interference from TV, or timing signals, as all the Hondas have problems with their electronics that day. The disappointment at Mugello is worse still, the only zero of the season, but this is tempered by victory in Barcelona, a clean win, apart from the commotion which follows it. The championship race has come well and truly alive.

The three Italians lead the world championship standings, with Rossi closing in on the title with more than a race to spare. Assen, with its magnificent bends, is the theatre for an eagerly awaited showdown, but yet again the rain sets in. Capirossi (who immediately breaks away), Biaggi, who leads in the central part of the race, and Rossi, who takes the lead just before the first downpour, prepare for a nail-biting finish. Biaggi, with a little luck and intuition, retakes the lead. Then the heavens really open, freezing the leader board and denying the fans what would have been the three best laps of the championship. Max wins, this time without controversy, flanked on the podium by Valentino and Loris. Then comes the British GP, where Capirossi leaves the other two Italians to fight it out.

On the Donington circuit, where the year before he won his first race in 500cc, Rossi takes his revenge on Biaggi, resolving an embarrassing situation with determination. Practice had been fairly disastrous (11th, after falling off on Friday), and the race is running away from him with Max

FIRST BEND OF CATALAN GP: VALENTINO HAS TO LIFT UP TO AVOID GOING OFF. HE BRUSHES THE SPANIARD CRIVILLE (28) AND FALLS BACK

16th PLACE, THEN STAGES A GREAT COMEBACK TO WIN

I MANAGED TO REMAIN CALM AND WAITED A LITTLE BEFORE STARTING MY COMEBACK

CATALAN GP

A BIKE HAS A SOUL, YOU'VE GOT TO UNDERSTAND IT. BUT IT'S FEMALE AND, LIKE ALL WOMEN, IT CAN LIFT YOU UP BUT ALSO LET YOU DOWN

VALENTINO ROSSI CHASED BY THE REIGNING CHAMPION, THE AMERICAN KENNY ROBERTS. COMPARED WITH 2000 THINGS HAVE CHANGED. ROSSI IS THE NEW KING OF THE SENIOR CLASS, WHILE TH

CALIFORNIAN MUST MAKE DO: HE WILL ONLY FINISH ON THE PODIUM IN VALENCIA

shooting off from pole. But Valentino manages a wonderful comeback – 'My best race so far in 500' – to win. Max is unhappy: 'If someone starts from the third row of the grid and then comes back to win, it means that there is something wrong.' The Roman rider is disappointed with his bike, which has given him trouble all year, but the Yamaha allows him to pull off the coup of the season in the very next race: he dominates the German GP, winning on a black day for Rossi, who finishes 7th on a track he has never liked. The gap narrows dramatically.

Just 10 points, when the whole second half of the season – 7 GPs – is still to be raced.

This is where 'The Doctor' produces perhaps his finest ever work, embarking on a relentless pursuit of the title. He wins every race, with the exception of a chaotic affair in Valencia, where the rain yet again wreaks havoc and riders play roulette with their choice of dry- or wet-weather tyres. The result is no Italians on the podium and Sete Gibernau's first win – hailed at the time as the start of a comeback but subsequently to prove just a flash in the pan.

Before Valencia Rossi produces a towering performance in Estoril, beating a very stubborn Capirossi, and follows it with another *tour de force* at Motegi, where Biaggi doubles his stakes, but loses everything. Max chooses a 17-inch rear tyre to gain a fast start and hopefully an unassailable lead, but Rossi realises and, for once, starts strongly. A duel ensues between the two racing gladiators, ending with five laps to go when Max flies off.

The championship is Valentino's for the taking. He could play safe at the Australian GP, seven days later, and make sure

46
THE DOCTOR
ENERGIE
BREIL
WATCHES
MANPOWER
domino
HONDA
VALE46
MICHELIN

WHY SO FEW POINTS FOR THE WINNER?
BRITISH GP (WINNER)

of putting points on the board, but he rejects the idea out of hand: 'I race to win, not to finish eighth.' And that is how it turns out: Valentino is fully committed from the start, despite the risks. Nearing the home straight, his rival Max is in the lead and Valentino could afford to let him win, it would not change anything, but at the little downhill bend near the finish line, where you overtake on the inside, he gets past on the outside in a thrilling manoeuvre. His line on the next bend is not quite as perfect and Biaggi goes all out to take back the lead, but in vain. Rossi wins by 13 thousandths of a second, or by 79 cm, on the line.

Capirossi is third, completing the most perfect podium of an exhilarating championship. Amid the scenes of celebration, mum Stefania sheds a few tears, having 'travelled 20,000 kms just to see me on television'. Dad Graziano, meanwhile, minus his trademark plait, having had it chopped off back in Tavullia, declared simply: 'It was worth it.' There is also time for Valentino to get a custard pie in the face from ex-rider Randy Mamola after the press conference. And then comes the coronation, when he is handed the world title by Mick Doohan, his predecessor in more ways than one, and Franco Uncini, the last Italian champion.

After so many thrills and so much excitement, and the dream-like result at Philip Island, the race for the year's world championship is over. But Valentino is like another legend of two wheels, Eddy Merckx – he devours opponents and always wants to win – and there are another two races to increase his points tally. The hardest thing is to maintain concentration, most of all for the team, which, having achieved its target now starts to relax. This does not apply to Valentino, though, it is

 THE PRODIGY SHOWS OFF IN A BURN-OUT. LOTS OF SMOKE TO CELEBRATE THE END OF A RACE – A REAL CROWD-PLEASER. ROSSI KEEPS THE CROWD HAPPY, EVEN IF THE TYRES ARE NOT...

46

agv
46
ENERGIE
46
Birra · Beer
Nastro Azzurro
HRC
polini
BREIL
MANPOWER
domino
HONDA
PlayStation.2
Birra · Beer
Nastro Azzurro
Expert Lager
polini
MICHELIN
brembo
NGK
AFAM
RK
BIOFOX
REPSOL YPF
Beta
VALE 46
HONDA

46
agv
'EN<RGIE
46
HONDA
BREIL
domino
HONDA
PlayStation 2
NSR
polini
Bina · Beer
Nastro Azzurro
brembo
MICHELIN
NGK
AFAM
BIOFOX
Verlicchi
SHOWA
DAINESE
HONDA
polini
Bina · Beer
Nastro Azzurro

A CHAIN OF JAPANESE BIKES: VALENTINO'S HONDA LEADS THE YAMAHAS OF CARLOS CHECA AND MAX BIAGGI

simply not in his character. So there is another surge to beat Capirossi emphatically in Malaysia, and Checa in Rio, where he even manages to win after crossing the line second. Because of yet more rain, the race is decided on the sum of times in a two-part race, and the advantage accumulated in the first part sees him finish considerably quicker than the Spaniard. A victory which is worth double, as it allows him to give a fitting send-off to his great love: The Honda NSR 500, the bike he always dreamed of riding from his first lap on a minimoto. The machine Rossi called 'the most exciting bike I have ever ridden' is to be replaced due to the introduction of four-stroke engines. A new era begins, and with it comes a new challenge.

ARMS RAISED ALOFT IN VICTORY, A COMMON SCENE WHEN VALENTINO IS RACING: 11 WINS IN 2001

ROSSI, **KING** OF A NEW ERA

Try to imagine the scene. It is Tuesday 7 August 2001 and there is a posse of Japanese engineers waiting in the pits, a mixture of satisfaction and pride on their faces. Valentino Rossi gets off the new RC211V he has been testing, a jewel of a bike. You can hear a pin drop, and the Italian says straight off the bat: 'That's it, you guys can race it.' Suddenly there is a look of despair on the assembled faces, as the Japanese try to remain impassive. Thus begins the era of four-stroke engines and the plans for Rossi's 2002 season.

The man from Tavullia was already in a bad mood, having spent several days at Suzuka when he could have been at the beach. He was also tired because of the Suzuka 8 Hours endurance race (though satisfied by his win with Colin

7 AUGUST 2001: VALENTINO MAKES HIS DEBUT WITH THE NE

ONDA RC211V ON THE SUZUKA TRACK. HIS TEAM MATE IS UKAWA (11)

IF THE FOUR-STROKES ARE 2-3 SECONDS SLOWER THAN THE TWO-STROKES, I'D BE HAPPY. IF WE ARE ONE SECOND SLOWER IT'D BE A MIRACLE

HE STRUGGLES TO ADJUST TO THE RC211V. IN PRE-SEASON TESTS, VALE IS CRITICAL OF THE JAPANESE FOUR-STROKE: 'I'LL CRY WHEN I RIDE IT. THIS WAY WE'LL LOSE REAL BIKES. THESE ARE FAST, BUT THE

ON'T GIVE THE SAME FEELING OF POWER AS TWO-STROKES. THE NEW BIKE WEARS THE TYRES TOO MUCH. I WANT THE OLD ONE BACK'

Edwards) and, as always, irritated by the tests. The bike was still a long way from being able to replace the thrill of his beloved NSR 500, which was at the same time taking him to his third world championship title. But the good pro that he is, he knuckles down with Jeremy Burgess and produces a very long 'wish list' of modifications and complete changes he wants.

This story should have resumed in January, when the first tests of the new bike are scheduled in Australia, but again, not everything goes according to plan. This time it is not the engineers' fault, but the managers'. Valentino's contract is under renewal and, just when everything seems to be in place, the negotiations fall apart, leaving the two sides at loggerheads. Only those directly involved know exactly what happened, but Honda make it clear to Rossi that until he signs the contract, he is not getting on the bike.

Finally the signature is secured, but the magic spell that bound the two has been broken. Nonetheless, the remarkable sequence of victories that follows leaves no room for lingering bitterness. The season becomes an unqualified triumph – 11 wins, 4 second places and one withdrawal for technical reasons – achieved thanks to a rider in superlative form, and a perfect bike that seems to have been beamed down from another planet.

Of course, credit must go to those engineers at Suzuka who, after receiving the initial body blow of their driver's assessment, went to work immediately on rectifying the situation. Valentino, much to his credit, is the first to pay tribute to their exemplary work: 'They did everything I asked of them. They made an incredible effort and now the bike is performing very well. I'm still excited when I think of the thrills I got from the 500cc bike, but I must admit that these four-strokes have incredible performance.' The class was different, but the outcome would be the same, with Rossi clearly embarking on a love affair with his new bike.

There is nothing left to do but start winning, and what better occasion than at Honda's home Grand Prix in Suzuka? Valentino, apart from being a great rider, is also extremely clever. He knows that some victories are worth double, and the Japanese race is perhaps worth even more. So the first GP of the four-stroke era becomes one of those events not to be missed under any circumstances. This revolution has been too important for the chance to be squandered. Honda were, a few years earlier, the most steadfast in demanding this great change. Eco-industrial problems lead to the decision to gradually move their entire global production from two-stroke to four-stroke and racing was to be the spearhead of this transformation, despite the enormous expenditure.

Their engineers, in order to avoid the risk of being shown up, even manage to get the regulations changed – allowing the engine capacity to be doubled – so that the old 500s would not stand a chance. There would be no contest in this unique transition season, with the two-stroke's only chance of a win coming in Germany.

IN JEREZ VALE MAKES UP FOR SOUTH AFRICA WITH AN EMPHATIC WIN OVER KATO (74). AFTER THRE

I WON, BUT I'M NOT HAPPY. AFTER THE RACE I SAW LAZIO-INTER LIVE IN MY MOTORHOME. I CAN'T BELIEVE WE LOST THE SCUDETTO LIKE THAT

SPANISH GP (5 MAY 2002)

RACES MOTOGP ALREADY HAS A MASTER: VALE LEADS WITH 29 POINTS (TWO WINS AND A SECOND PLACE) AHEAD OF UKAWA

REPSOL
REPSOL
GAS
MANPOWER
NGK
SPARK
PLUGS
REPSOL
HONDA
46
agv
agv
REPSOL
GAS
THE DOCTOR
GAS

REPSOL
HRC
HONDA RACING
REPSOL
GAS
MANPOWER
HONDA
REPSOL
GAS
MICHELIN
agv
TRIBÙ DEL CHIHUAHUA
BLUE JEANS GAS
HONDA
REPSOL
GAS

46
46
46
46
46
46
46
46
46
46
46
46
46
46
46
46
46
46
46
46

ITALIAN GP AT MUGELLO: THE STANDS BECOME A SEA OF YELLOW PLACARDS BEARING VALE'S NUMBER – 46

THEY'RE OFF: ROSSI AND BIAGGI IN THE LEAD. THE ETERNAL DERBY BETWEEN THE TWO ITALIAN

ACES CONTINUES. VALE WINS: 'I LET HIM DO HIS THING FOR A BIT, THEN I TOOK THE LEAD. MY BIKE HAS A BIT EXTRA'

The imbalance between MotoGP and 500cc racing is exemplified by Loris Capirossi's performance in the South African GP. On a track favourable to the old bikes, he went flat out and finished 16 seconds quicker than in 2001 . . . but still only managed third spot behind two RCVs. If there was to be a revolution, Rossi was going to lead it. So at Suzuka he takes no prisoners, despite the rain. Local rider Akira Ryo gave Vale a run for his money. He was one of those wild cards Valentino learned to recognise when he raced in 125, riders who are ready to sell their soul to the devil for success on their home track, and who know all the tricks of the circuit. Still and all it was not enough for the local rider.

It should have been a party, but yet again there is controversy – not wholly unexpected it should be said. During the lap of honour someone hands Rossi a Honda flag, which somehow never makes it onto the podium. 'It's nicer to wave the Italian flag when I win. This time I took the Honda flag, but "unfortunately" I dropped it,' quips the Italian. Later, in the press conference, there is more controversy instead of celebration. The team manager, Noriaki Nakata, is asked whether this first win for the four-stroke bike is down to Rossi, but he answers by lavishing praise on the Honda racing division without mentioning Valentino at all. Feeling insulted, Rossi offers his own version: 'They only want to highlight the bike and make sure it's not overshadowed by me. They can't have taken kindly to the fact that last year we gave their official riders a kicking with a satellite team. I'm sure that by mid-season they'll give my bike to Kato too, despite the fact that he's not in the official team.'

More controversy follows shortly after. In the next race he

Servizio di Vigilanza Urbana — Pesaro

SOMMARIO PROCESSO VERBALE N°

Oggi 2/6/2002 ore 14.15 Via/Piazza

al Signor ROSSI VALENTINO

nato il 16/2/79 a URBINO

residente a TAVULLIA Via

patente: cat. B N. 1246 Pref. il

conducente del veicolo tipo HONDA RC211V

telaio N. 46 motore N. targa

libretto N. I.M.C.T.C.

il di proprietà

nato il a

residente a Via

viene contestata la violazione al C. d. S. qui sotto indicata con la «X»:

- ☐ veicolo mancante del silenziatore (art.47 C. d. S.);
- ☒ veicolo con silenziatore di tipo non approvato (art. 47 C. d. S.);
- ☐ veicolo con silenziatore alterato (art. 112 C. d. S.);
- ☐ veicolo con silenziatore in palesi condizioni di inefficienza (art. 112 C. d. S.);
- ☒ veicolo con freni stridenti (art. 112 C. d. S.);
- ☒ veicolo mancante del dispositivo di segnalazione acustica (art. 46 C. d. S.);
- ☐ veicolo con dispositivo di segnalazione acustica di tipo non approvato (art. 46 C. d. S.);
- ☒ SORPASSO A DESTRA AGGRAVATO DALLA VICINANZA DELLA CURVA

Il proprietario viene pertanto invitato a portare a revisione il veicolo presso l'I.M.C.T.C. di TAVULLIA, da lui stesso prescelto.

Il Trasgressore dichiara:

Il Trasgressore

L'Agente Accertatore

Oblazione: entro 15 giorni da oggi L.

dal 16° al 60° giorno

Consegnata copia al trasgressore e al proprietario del veicolo

Pagato L. ; Libro N. ; Bolletta N. N. del registro

THE ITALIAN GP IS OVER, THE PARTY BEGINS: TWO POLICEMEN STOP HI

OR OVERTAKING ON THE OUTSIDE, BUT IT IS JUST A JOKE ORGANISED BY THE FAN CLUB

 IN INIMITABLE STYLE, VALE CELEBRATES HIS 46TH WIN IN HIS 100TH GP

ECSTATIC ROSSI SITS SIDEWAYS ACROSS THE FUEL TANK. BIAGGI, 2ND, PASSES TOO CLOSE WITH HIS YAMAHA: MORE CONTROVERSY

suffers his only 'defeat' (for anyone else, second place would be a reason to celebrate). The head-to-head with team-mate and journeyman rider Tohru Ukawa seems to leave the Japanese with no chance. Things are fine when Valentino is out in front, but when Ukawa leads, the rhythm drops, or rather, it plummets. The less risky option seems to be trying to lead from the front as opposed to surging through the back markers, but he can't quite shake off his rival. Then at the last abrupt braking point on the last lap Valentino's RCV loses its line, leaving the road open to Ukawa. The Japanese rider's smile is the same one he had at Castellet in 1999, when a problem with Vale's bike gifted him the first win of his career. This one would be the last.

For Rossi, on the other hand, it is his first defeat of the season. In nine races, i.e. up until Germany, the last GP before the summer break, he notches up an incredible eight wins. This run practically secures him the title, thanks to the 96-point lead he has on the chasing pack with 'only' seven races to go. There then follows a memorable string of victories: a smooth performance at Jerez, where the only scare comes with a surge from Kenny Roberts; a surprising win at Le Mans, where the race is stopped early due to rain – 'The defeat at Assen in 2001 taught me to stay up front when the weather closes in. But I don't like winning like this,' the Italian said of the triumph. After that he has a victory to savour at Mugello, in spite of a difficult start in front of his people. Earlier he had destroyed the best bike in the warm up: certainly not a good start to a Sunday of racing, given that he fell off twice there the previous year.

In Tuscany, he executes an opportunistic overtaking

AT THE SACHSENRING, ALEX BARROS KNOCKS OLIVIER JACQUE OVER WITH THREE LAPS TO GO. VALENTINO SAYS THANK YOU VERY MUCH AND WINS HIS EIGHTH RACE OF NINE: 96 POINTS AHEAD OF TOHRU UKA

manoeuvre on his rival Max Biaggi at the Casanova-Savelli, where the two opposing sets of fans have taken positions. Then comes the fantastic set-piece with the policemen giving him a fine. It is so realistic that his grandmother, watching on TV, calls the circuit to find out what has happened. He goes on to win in Barcelona and is again involved in a heated post-race exchange that inevitably involves Biaggi. 'The Yamaha goes like my Honda,' said Rossi after the race. 'With the bike he has he shouldn't say these things,' comes the retort from Max. At Assen, he draws on his reserves of strength to beat Barros – 'I've never seen anyone go as fast as Alex did today,' Rossi would say afterwards – thanks to two hellish laps towards the end of the race. His win at Donington comes with a new record. Fittingly it had to be there on the same circuit where he won his first race in 500cc, back in 2000. When Valentino senses he has a date with destiny, or history for that matter, you can be sure he will arrive on time. In England this meant overcoming a bang to the head in testing, which caused him to miss the first day of qualifying, before going on to take pole. In the race Carlos Checa tries to slow him down until the Spaniard skids off. It is a victory that is worth double because the chasing Ukawa is in hospital, blocked by a fall he suffered on Friday morning, two minutes before Rossi's, but a lot more serious. There is also the symbolic value of it being career win

19
GO!!!!!!
YAMAHA
agv
REPSOL
GAS
MANPOWER
46
REPSOL
GAS
MICHELIN
HONDA

Marlboro
SUOMY
YAMAHA
Marlboro
MOTUL
YAMAHA
MOTUL
46

*IT WAS LIKE BLOWING
A TYRE ON THE MOTORWAY,
BUT LUCKILY I DIDN'T COME OFF.
THIS SETBACK HURTS BECAUSE
IT WASN'T MY FAULT*

CZECH REPUBLIC GP

ROSSI IS LET DOWN IN THE 16TH LAP BY THE REAR TYRE. HE IS FORCED TO RETIRE

number 46 (his racing number) in his 100th GP. As if this were not enough, it is also win number 100 for chief engineer Jeremy Burgess.

It is a triumph tainted by the now customary squabbling: while Rossi is celebrating under a chequered flag bearing his number – sitting across the fuel tank like a mother on a Vespa in the 1960s – Biaggi shoots past him at over 200 km/h, far too close for safety. The champion claims it was out of spite – 'He hates it because I always beat him' – while the Roman says he had no choice in the matter – 'I was still in the race and had to maintain my lead over Barros.' Angry words, then a qualified apology from Rossi. It is business as usual.

Like in the win at the Sachsenring, the only track where a two-stroke could really have beaten the new bikes, Valentino has to be on his best form to stay in touch, especially after his slow start. In the end, though, it is a dismal performance from Barros that hands victory on a plate to Rossi. With the race reaching its conclusion and the battle getting intense, Alex gets his braking wrong on the finish straight and collides with Olivier Jacque, the other rider in contention for the win. Vale can go on holiday safe in the knowledge that his fifth title is in the bag.

The newly crowned champion faces a reality check when they return to the track. The venue is Brno, where Biaggi reigns, and the racing world once again witnesses barbed comments, half-accusations (not just from the Roman rider) and claims about having a bike that can win on its own – a particularly sensitive issue, which begins to get under Valentino's skin. But the incredible showdown is brought to an abrupt end seven laps from the end by the sound of rubber ripping apart the mudguard and tailpiece of his bike. Though doubtless caused by a tyre defect, it is a slice of bad luck that can never be fully explained, and the spectacle is cut short.

HE TRIUMPHS IN THE RAIN IN RIO: AFTER 125CC, 250CC AND 500CC, THE MOTOGP TITLE IS HIS TOO

REPSOL
GAS
GASJEANS.COM
DAINESE
pollini

AND IT'S FOUR. MAX BIAGGI JOINS THE PARTY ON THE PODIUM. VALENTINO ROSSI IS SOAKED IN CHAMPAGNE

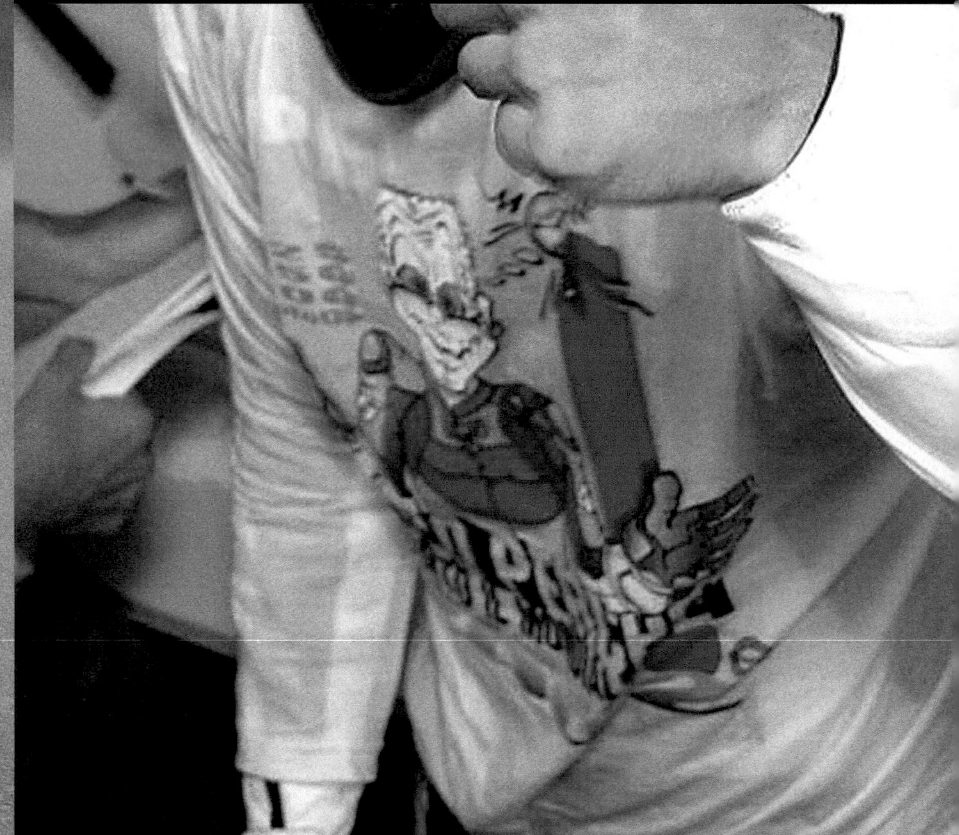

I'M REALLY LUCKY: THE LAST CHAMPION IN 500CC AND THE FIRST IN THE HISTORY OF MOTOGP

RIO GP

HE ROMAN POURS AN ENTIRE BOTTLE OVER HIM. THE HAPPIER SIDE OF AN HISTORIC RIVALRY

THE MOTOGP FIELD IN ACTION AT SEPANG IN THE MALAYSIAN GP. BIAGGI IS PARTICULARLY INSPIRED AND WINS, ROSSI MUST MAKE DO WITH SECOND PLACE. AND MAX REVEALS: 'THANK YOU YAMAHA, EVEN

E WON'T BE TOGETHER NEXT YEAR. ROSSI?' VALE ACCUSES UKAWA: 'HE GOT UP TO ALL SORTS'

AT PHILIP ISLAND, ROSSI RETURNS TO VICTORY. IT'S THE THIRD OF THE FOUR RACES OF THE MINI-WORLD CHAMPIONSHIP, A HONDA DERBY WITH ALEX BARROS. VALE IS BEATEN IN THE END. THE BRAZILIA

IT'S A PITY BARROS MADE THAT MISTAKE AT THE END. WE WOULD HAVE OVERTAKEN EACH OTHER 3-4 TIMES, BUT I'D HAVE STILL BEATEN HIM

AUSTRALIAN GP

VINS THE LAST RACE IN VALENCIA, AND TAKES THE TITLE WITH 86 POINTS, ONE AHEAD OF ROSSI

'I had the best Biaggi of the last three years ahead of me, I didn't know how it would end up, but I kept on trying until the end.' As it transpires, this momentary disappointment proves no more than a small diversion on the open road to the world title. Preparation for this takes place in the pouring rain in Estoril. 90 falls in 3 days, including 53 during the GP (of which 8 came in the senior class) are testimony to the treacherous conditions. On the track, long-time race leader Sete Gibernau is forced out by a technical problem with his Suzuki, which hands another victory to Valentino. The Italian then finds the right gear in Brazil, where it is raining once again, securing victory and another world title after a breathtaking series of moves. The feat elicits praise even from long time nemesis Biaggi, who spent the whole season trying to spoil Vale's party, succeeding only in delaying his coronation by one GP. 'Rossi has had an excellent championship, he was good and deserves the title,' admits Max. For Rossi, it is wonderful, even better than the party with Tavullia's version of the Brazil football team lifting a fake world cup for the fourth title, one less than the footballing legends.

The rest is academic. The Mundialito sees a half-hearted contest with Alex Barros, who has ridden an RCV like his since the Motegi race. The Brazilian beats him in Japan. Biaggi wins in Malaysia, with Rossi and Alex on the podium. In Australia, Valentino takes his revenge to secure his 50th win, saying: 'When I read that Doohan managed this feat, I never thought I'd match it.' Still the Brazilian is snapping at his heels. The mini championship, which nobody was too bothered about, ends in Valencia, with another win for Barros. It is a small consolation for Valentino's long-suffering rival, but there is only one real legend: with four world titles in four different categories, there is nobody like Rossi.

I'VE WON MY 50th RACE: A DREAM.
IN 1998 I READ THAT DOOHAN REACHED 50
WINS. I ASKED MYSELF IF I'D EVER GET THERE

AUSTRALIAN GP

THE SAME OLD **FANTASTIC** VALENTINO

VALENTINO AND MAX BIAGGI, THE CONTEST CONTINUES IN 2003

Nine victories, five second places and two third places from 16 races with the all-time points record in the history of the senior class. These raw statistics might have you believe that the 2003 season was a boring Rossi victory parade, with no contest and no thrills. But it was nothing of the sort. 2003 played out amid painful tears, drama, anger, exuberance, controversy, and excitement, and is remembered as a great championship season and one worthy of bestowing a fifth world title on the man from Tavullia. The season would also be his final one with Honda before switching to Yamaha, a move unprecedented in motorcycling racing and one that would define an era.

The season starts badly, however, with a scare after Marco Melandri flies off, before a tragic accident at the wonderful, yet cursed, Suzuka track claims the life of the top-rated rider Daijiro Kato.

REPSOL

152 ROSSI WITH DAIJIRO KATO, THE JAPANESE RIDER WHO DIED TRAGICALLY AT SUZUKA

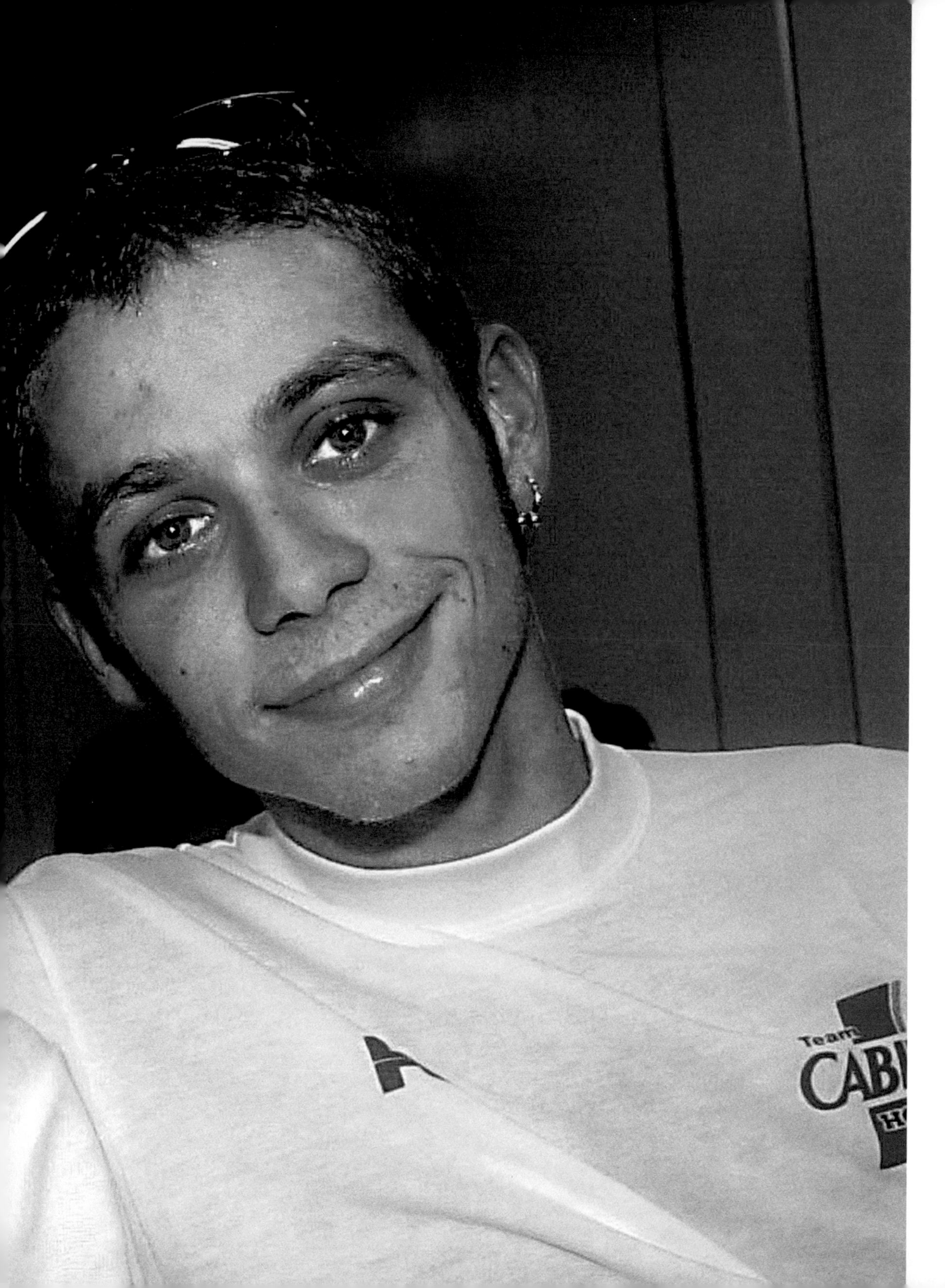

The death of the Japanese rider at Suzuka provided a timely wake-up call to motorcycle racing, in much the same way that Ayrton Senna's passing affected Formula 1 in 1994. Riders, so often used to feeling invincible, are suddenly reminded of their vulnerability and the need to demand better safety measures.

This calls for the riders to speak as one and work, not against the system, but with it, in order to make their voices heard. On this occasion the loudest voice is that of the most talented rider, Rossi, who realises that as champion he has an obligation to represent his colleagues. In all there are four of them – Vale, the Spaniard Sete Gibernau, the American Kenny Roberts and Japan's Nobuatsu Aoki – who negotiate with Carmelo Ezpelata, head of the Dorna organisation, and Franco Uncini, the ex-world champion now head of safety. Together, they look at all the circuits, deciding where and how to intervene in order to improve the safety margins in case of an accident, something that could also make the difference between winning and losing a world title.

But most of all this is a season of tension. Vale's understanding with Honda has by now reached an end. His contract runs for another year, but the love between the two parties is gone. His nemesis Max Biaggi unwittingly gives him a hand in making his decision when he declares in Barcelona: 'He says he wants to change, but he'll never leave Honda. He is treated too well there and he doesn't have the balls to accept the Ducati challenge.' At the time, the red Italian bike is being mooted as Valentino's possible next ride, but behind the scenes, he is courting and being courted by Yamaha. It is a revelation that rocks the championship to its core and means nothing can be taken for granted regarding team selection for the forthcoming season.

CHIHUAHUA
arnette
AGV
Dainese
agv
dainese

ROSSI WITH AUSTRALIAN CHIEF ENGINEER JEREMY BURGESS: A WORLD CHAMPIONSHIP DUO

 VALENTINO THRILLS THE 73,000 FANS AT MUGELLO. THE PODIUM IS ALL-ITALIAN, WITH ROSSI AHEAD OF LORIS AND MAX. IN THE 5th RACE OF THE SEASON, THE PRODIGY HAS ALREADY BROKEN AWAY WITH

I'M LIKE SCHUMI

ITALIAN GP

2-POINT LEAD OVER BIAGGI. BUT IN THE ITALIAN GP HIS TOUGHEST ADVERSARY IS CAPIROSSI: 'IN THE HEAT' – SAYS VALE – 'I SAW THE MADONNA. I PUSHED UNTIL THE LAST TO BEAT THE DUCATI'

THE RACE STARTS, BIAGGI IS WAY BACK. THIS TIME THE THREAT IS CAPIROSSI

WITH ROSSI IN THE SAND I DIDN'T RELAX, I CONTINUED TO RIDE LIKE A MADMAN. I DIDN'T WANT TO LOOK BEHIND ME

LORIS CAPIROSSI (CATALAN GP)

Controversy follows, with statements and accusations flying around, some claiming that Honda are too strong and that anyone could win on their bikes.

Rossi is not happy and makes his feelings known on more than one occasion: 'If Ferrari dominates, everyone says that Schumacher is a great driver. But me, I don't count for anything here.' For a natural talent like Valentino, capable of winning with all types of bikes and engines, often in quick succession, this is unacceptable. He puts his point across in his own inimitable style, with a set-piece at Brno based on an image of Valentino doing hard labour, 'condemned' to win so as not to hear grumbling over his shoulder about second places. The situation is tense, with malicious gossip circulating that Rossi is 'playing cat and mouse' and 'only wins when he wants to'. But what else is he to do? The best rider, with the best bike, assisted by the best team is always going to wipe the board with the competition.

Some victories come easily, but when it comes to knuckling down Valentino shows again he has what it takes. At the Spanish GP in Barcelona, back when Loris Capirossi was still at his magical best on the Ducati, the champion is involved in a thrilling battle for the lead with him and Biaggi. Rossi gets a bit too close to the Ducati rider and ends up on the grass to avoid colliding. He comes back on in fifth position, nine seconds behind Capirossi – surely an impossible gap to make up, what with only nine laps to go and Capirossi riding the best he had ever ridden in senior class. In the end it proves too big an ask, but Rossi still finishes second after a breathtaking series of overtaking manoeuvres that sees him close the gap on the leader to just three seconds. 'Another five laps and I'd have taken Capirossi

HE CLASSIC RACE AT ASSEN IS RUINED BY RAIN. THE WET TRACK MAKES EVERYTHING MORE DIFFICULT, FROM TYRE CHOICE TO VISIBILITY. THE ITALIANS FACE A CHALLENGE FROM GIBERNAU

NOW I KNOW I CAN CHALLENGE ROSSI
GIBERNAU (DUTCH GP)

BIAGGI AND ROSSI ON THE PODIUM, BUT AT ASSEN THEY MUST MAKE DO WITH 2nd AND 3rd

CONTROVERSIAL END TO THE BRITISH GP AT DONINGTON. VALENTINO DOMINATES, BUT PICKS UP 10 SECOND PENALTY AND IS RELEGATED TO 3rd PLACE AFTER OVERTAKING CAPIROSSI WITH A YELLOW FLAG SHOWING

I DIDN'T SEE THE
YELLOW FLAG. THEY USED
UNDERHAND TACTICS

BRITISH GP

too,' Valentino claimed, and it was probably no idle boast. Later at the Japanese Grand Prix in Motegi, with Biaggi his main adversary, he once again comes within a whisker of pulling off a famous win on a track he has never liked. Asked at the time if he felt he was unbeatable if he didn't make a mistake, Rossi had the humility to reply: 'I don't know.'

Another slip-up ensues in Japan, followed by a phenomenal comeback (from 9th spot) to take second place on the podium and all but seal a fifth title.

But the real master-class in clever riding and indomitable determination comes in Australia. The title is already won, but Vale's thirst for victory is insatiable. He finishes second, behind a fantastic Marco Melandri, but in front of Loris Capirossi. There is a real battle between the three and, when Troy Bayliss falls off at the hairpin, the fans' hearts skip a collective beat. Biaggi is adversely affected by the accident, which forces him off the track, causing him to fall. Valentino's problems begin on the next lap when he illegally passes Melandri with the yellow flag still shown. 'I didn't see it', he would claim later, 'this is turning into a real problem.'

There is a delay before the race directors, who have either missed the incident or cannot agree on their sanction, come down hard on the champion, issuing a 10-second penalty in the 12th lap (7 after the incident), with just 15 more to race. It takes a couple of laps for Vale to understand what has happened – the only means of communication is the pit wall board – and then he starts a race against the clock the likes of which has never been seen before. Rossi dictates an unbelievably quick tempo, which Capirossi is unable to match or do anything about, and amazingly finishes five seconds ahead even after the penalty has been deducted. 'I didn't think I could go

THE DUCATI IS THE REVELATION OF THIS SEASON. ON THE STRAIGHTS IT IS 10 KM/H FASTER

65
46
99
REPSOL

A BUCKET OF WATER IN MID-AUGUST AT BRNO. ROSSI RETURNS TO VICTORY IN THE CZECH REPUBLIC GP

FTER FOUR RACES WITHOUT A WIN

IT'S TIME TO PARTY, BUT THERE IS ALSO A DOUBLE-EDGED MESSAGE FOR HONDA: 'I DEVELOPED THE RC211V, SO WHY GIVE TAMADA THE SAME BIKE?' LATER, ON THE RENEWAL OF HIS CONTRACT, VALE WARN

HE JAPANESE TEAM: 'THERE IS NOBODY IN THE WORLD WHO CAN BEAT ME NOW.' THE TITLE IS EVER CLOSER: HE HAS A 51-POINT LEAD OVER GIBERNAU

that quickly,' he said at the end, after perhaps his best ever performance on a Honda. His happiness was in contrast with his dark mood three months previously at Donington, when the yellow flags first became an issue.

As always it is a great race at Donington, on a brilliant track where he has already won 5 times, including the first, unforgettable victory with the NSR 500.

The race starts off in chaos with the usual bottleneck at the first bend. Bikes knock against each other and Tohru Ukawa comes off. At the following bend the group is still closely packed, with the riders shooting through in quick succession. Biaggi leads, taking the role of the hare, Capirossi is fourth, while Rossi immediately finds himself chasing. He starts a charge and overtakes at the very point where the accident happened and where the clear-up is almost complete. Unfortunately the yellow flags are still being waved, or rather one yellow flag.

The race directors do not move an inch – someone points out what has happened and questions start being asked. But all this happens far from the track, obviously, where Max and Valentino are busy with one of their exciting duels. The Roman rider leads, with Rossi hugging the bends to put pressure on his rival. He manages to slip past at the S-bend which divides the fast part of the track from the sequence of bends at the end. Biaggi loses his shape and his line, Rossi overtakes and prepares for another triumphant gallop to the finish. But there is a sting in the tail. After three hours of discussions, the race directors come up with a decision: a 10-second retrospective penalty 'because considering the 20 laps remaining and the pace of the race, if he (Rossi) had known of the penalty, he would have gone that fast to make up the time, etc, etc, etc . . .' Still, the victory is Biaggi's – at least according to the officials – although the Roman rider is reluctant to celebrate, saying: 'I understand how he

Nastro Azzurro
CAMEL
GAS
GAS

HE EVE OF THE MALAYSIAN GP IS A SPECIAL MOMENT FOR VALENTINO ROSSI. AT SEPANG THE MAN FROM TAVULLIA GETS HIS FIRST OPPORTUNITY TO TIE UP THE WORLD TITLE . . . AND REFUSES TO LET IT SLIP AWAY

feels, I've experienced this too.' Of course, Rossi never asks for the winner's trophy back, as there is no way he would have handed it back if the roles had been reversed.

The season is an Italian duel that more than once turns into Italian domination. From the start, in the tragic race at Suzuka when Valentino celebrated on the podium unaware of what had befallen poor Kato, Rossi is flanked by Max and Loris, the Ducati managing a podium finish at the first attempt, in the enemy's backyard in Japan. The home GP, at a sell-out Mugello circuit, is much more exciting, although there is only ever going to be one winner. Valentino dominates, while Loris and Max are involved in a great duel that sees Capirossi overtaking Biaggi at the end of the straight and the two almost face to face as the Ducati cut across the Yamaha's path. The manoeuvre is incredible, as is the sea of crazy fans that swamps Valentino, first on the track during a risky lap of honour, and then on the podium, giving him what he described as a 'fantastic thrill'.

Valentino wins again in Portugal, where the all-Italian podium is repeated, but with Loris and Max swapping positions. Rossi finishes well ahead of the field, something that does not happen all that often. Biaggi is a comfortable second, while Capirossi shows determination in denying Gibernau third by a few thousandths of a second.

The Spaniard, who is a revelation this season, is becoming a real thorn in the champion's side. Valentino is served notice of his fighting spirit at the South African GP when, still mourning the death of his team-mate and friend Daijiro Kato, Sete manages an emphatic performance. But Gibernau is not a problem at the Spanish GP at Jerez where, much to the home crowd's disappointment, he succumbs to the pressure and takes an early fall off his new bike.

Valentino tries to avoid taking unnecessary risks. He breaks away in races and in the championship giving his opponents practically no chance of reply. However, one such opportunity falls to Sete Gibernau in the next race, in France. Le Mans is a track that Rossi has never loved, but the perfect combination of his riding talent and the strength of the Honda RC211V resolves this small obstacle.

Once again he breaks away for the win, opening up a 4-second gap on the group. Everything is under control, apart from the weather. With 12 laps to go the rain starts lashing down violently, causing the race to be stopped then restarted. However, there is no sum of times, to avoid a situation where the first across the line is not the winner.

agv
THE DOCTOR
HONDA
REPSOL
46
REPSOL
GAS
MANPOWER
REPSOL
HONDA
SHOWA
GAS
MICHELIN
NGK
RK
brembo

HONDA
REPSOL
46
SHOWA

THE DOCTOR
HONDA
46
REPSOL
HRC

 ROSSI ARRIVES AT PHILIP ISLAND WITH THE TITLE IN THE BAG

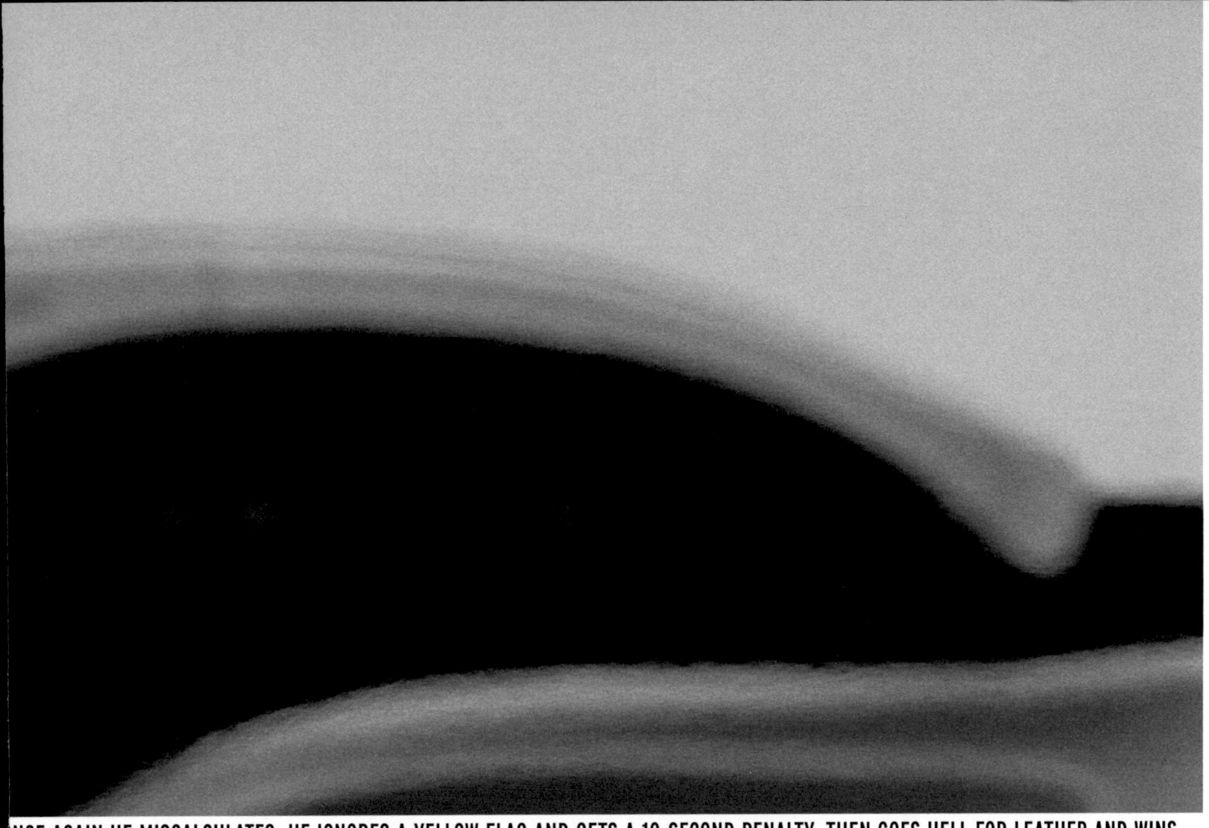

When the race starts again, the conditions look to favour Sete, who dictates the race (or what is left of it), but Rossi holds on. The last lap is a classic: Valentino attacks, the Spaniard holds him off, until the last bend where Rossi for a second gets a wheel ahead, but he cannot keep the line. He finishes second, but under the circumstances he is happy with that. The same happens at Assen, again on a wet track and with no complaints. For once he can make do.

It is another thing entirely in Germany – this defeat really does hurt. Valentino talks about it at length, as if it is a stain on his soul that is difficult to remove. Half of Tavullia is there ready to celebrate, the priest Don Cesare and even a papier maché church steeple. The race goes as expected, with Rossi keeping his toughest adversary under control and making a final attack in front of where his friends had taken position. The only thing they had not banked on was Gibernau's fierce resolve not to be beaten that day. The champion described it thus: 'He was always right behind me, and at the last bend I defended myself by closing the line to deny him the chance of attacking. But on the exit from the bend I went wide and he passed me.' It is a bitter disappointment, which Rossi responds to in the only way he knows: by annihilating the opposition. Of the seven remaining races, he goes on to win six of them, only missing out at Motegi. That one went to Biaggi after a superb ride, earning him his first win for Honda (excluding the farce at Donington).

The Japanese Grand Prix at Montegi goes like a dream for Max. He is always in control, setting the pace, while Valentino misses out on fighting for the lead in the final stages due to a mistake caused by the rear tyre being a little too hard. Japan aside, it is six victories out of six for Rossi, each win enjoyable in its own way. There is revenge at Brno, where he frees himself from the nightmarish cycle of

I'VE NEVER HAD A RACE LIKE THAT BEFORE

AUSTRALIAN GP

BLUE
JEANS
GAS
THE DOCTOR
REPSOL
HONDA
REPSOL
REPSOL
agv

agv
GAS
POWER
GAS
MANPOWER
GAS
MICHELIN

E CELEBRATES THE VALENCIA WIN BY WEARING A JIMI HENDRIX WIG. VALENTINO EVEN MANAGES TO OUT-DO HIMSELF: WITH 357 POINTS HE BEATS HIS FANTASTIC SCORE OF 2002 BY TWO POINTS

 END OF SEASON PHOTO. VALENTINO ROSSI, MOTOGP CHAMPION, WITH THE OTHER WORLD TITLE WINNERS OF 2003. ON THE LEFT IS SAN

RINO RIDER MANUEL POGGIALI, CHAMPION WITH THE APRILIA 250, ON THE RIGHT IS SPANIARD DANIEL PEDROSA, KING OF THE 125

'defeats', a smooth win in Portugal, then victory in Rio amid renewed speculation about his move to Yamaha, which at that point is nearly sealed, even if Biaggi, Capirossi and the other riders refuse to believe it. Later there is the incredible chase at Philip Island, with the title already in the bag, and then the finale at Valencia, where he says a goodbye to Honda with a light heart and no tears. 'Maybe I'm crazy to leave,' he says, keeping the emotion in check. But the icing on the cake has to be the Sepang race, the day of his crowning. 'For once I didn't sleep a wink,' he would admit later. He had dominated the championship and the finishing line was in sight. Though there would have been other chances if he had needed them, with Valentino when opportunity comes knocking, it is usually a case of grabbing it with both hands. Just once before, in 125cc, did he fail to take full advantage of a championship 'match point'. This time, however, there is no mistake. He wins pole position on Saturday, sets the fastest lap and then goes on to win the race with a real show of force. After struggling slightly early on, he then shuts out Gibernau completely, not allowing his season-long adversary the slightest chance to rain on his parade. As ever, Rossi achieves victory in his own inimitable fashion and can rightfully reflect on a job well done. This latest success made it three world championships in succession in the senior class: one in 500cc and two in MotoGP with Honda, though his relationship with the Japanese team had by then gone from being a fantastic dream to an irritating burden. It was a case of mission accomplished, bring on the next challenge.

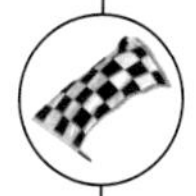

VALENTINO, THE **OSCAR** WINNING ACTOR

To the outside world it seemed a crazy decision, unfathomable. But he'd given it a lot of thought, perhaps more thought than he had ever given anything before. Suddenly he said: 'I've got to do it.' He could not bear to hear any more gossip about how easy everything was for him and how anyone could win with his Honda beneath them.

He knew that it was not true, but words are not enough for those who refuse to listen. Bold action was necessary, and that meant leaving the haughty environs of invincible Honda to join the competition and take up a difficult and exciting new challenge.

Before Rossi switched teams, Giacomo Agostini had tried something similar with a move from the four-stroke MV to the emerging two-stroke Yamahas. But this was more about the

KERA
GAULOISES
PIT-LANE
YAMAHA
GAULOISES

ROSSI GAINS CONFIDENCE WITH THE YAMAHA M1 IN PRE-SEASON TESTS. A FASCINATING CHALLENGE AWAITS HIM: TO BEAT 'HIS' HONDA RC211V, THE PERFECT BIKE. THE WORLD CHAMPION MOVES TO ANOTHE

PANESE BIKE, ONE WHICH DISAPPOINTED IN 2003 WITH JUST ONE PODIUM FOR ALEX BARROS. AT LE MANS, IN THE WET, THE BRAZILIAN FINISHES THIRD BEHIND GIBERNAU AND VALENTINO

I DIDN'T THINK I'D BE THE HARE

SOUTH AFRICAN GP

RST DAY OF TESTS AT WELKOM: ROSSI IS IMMEDIATELY FASTEST AND CELEBRATES WITH THE YAMAHA ENGINEERS. AMONG THESE, TO THE RIGHT OF VALE, IS TEAM MANAGER DAVIDE BRIVIO

VALENTINO ROSSI RELAXES IN THE YAMAHA PIT. IT IS THE SECOND RACE OF THE SEASON AND HE SUFFERS HIS FIRST DEFEAT.

GIBERNAU DOMINATES IN THE WET AND ROSSI FINISHES FOURTH

rider's foresight in predicting the end of a technical era and bravely leading the way.

Things were different now. The Honda had won 15 races out of 16 in 2003, dominating the championship like no other before it in the recent history of motorbike racing. Rossi was tempted by Ducati, with a sponsor who was willing to do anything for him, but they couldn't come to an agreement. And then there was the Yamaha, by then almost a derelict bike. But Valentino's keen judgment saw that the Japanese bike could be the ideal means of revenge. Only he believed in it. Even Honda, despite realising that the feel-good factor had gone, thought that in the end they would be able to hang on to him, more out of necessity than out of love. Nobody before had deserted Honda.

Rossi is an extraordinary rider, and always has been. So, seeing him in January 2005 with the emblems of the Iwata team may have seemed a little strange – but only up to a point. The betrayal came in a pit at Sepang, where he and Jeremy Burgess found themselves surrounded by a sea of Japanese engineers waiting for a response after a few laps to test the four-cylinder bike. 'There's work to be done, but it isn't bad' was Rossi's verdict. This marked the beginning of a famous coup, which would amaze everyone in the world of motorcycling . . . apart from Valentino and his team.

He is incredibly fast from the first tests, even though he must face up to new challenges. He holds up his creased hands with pride after a day spent on the track. The bike is difficult to control, but he knows how to tame it.

While the others rest unawares, Valentino prepares the deadliest of retributions. The good lap times he clocked up

RAIN INTERRUPTS THE RACE AT MUGELLO AS ROSSI LEADS. THE RACE IS RESTARTED – SIX MORE LAPS ON

I NEVER WANTED TO LEAVE THE PODIUM

ITALIAN GP

MP TRACK AND VALENTINO FINDS THE RIGHT GEAR TO LEAVE GIBERNAU BEHIND

196 ROSSI TRIUMPHS IN BARCELONA IN GIBERNAU'S HOME GP

I EVEN USED MY EARS TO BRAKE. MY ARMS NEARLY CAME OFF WITH THE EFFORT

CATALAN GP

in winter testing should have rung warning bells for his opponents – particularly when he won a BMW for a record lap in Barcelona. People thought the win was down to Valentino simply managing to use the bad weather to his advantage, rather than due to great progress in the development of the Yamaha. They were to be proved wrong.

At the start of the season in South Africa at Welkom, Rossi immediately shows how much the challenge means to him. In testing he quickly wins pole position, which is the prelude to a hard-fought race. It turns out to be a fittingly epic battle against Max Biaggi. The tension surrounding the contest finds its release in Valentino's boundless desire for victory: he is prepared to take any risks in order to win the race he has staked his career on. Even second place would be a triumph for Yamaha, but that means nothing to Rossi, who would prefer to fall off than suffer such an outcome. For Biaggi, the factors in play are different. He is not quite ready to risk everything and push the boundaries with an entire season ahead. For Rossi there is much more at stake, as witnessed by his joy on winning, when he stands exhausted before his beloved bike.

Honda was on its knees, beaten by a rider whom it had not appreciated enough – by a man who had proved that he was more important than the machine, as brilliant as it was. At that point Valentino could even have retired. He would thus have stolen the show in unprecedented fashion. Instead, though, he knuckled down for the hardest season of his career, and perhaps in motorcycle racing history. Can you go an entire championship riding to the limit, Sunday after Sunday? Many asked themselves this question, and not even

YAMAHA

'HAT AN EFFORT TO BEAT GIBERNAU.' ROSSI NEEDS TO BE ON TOP FORM YET AGAIN TO BEAT THE SPANIARD AT ASSEN WITH A DECISIVE MOVE IN THE RUN UP TO THE FINISH

Rossi could answer them. He would, however, find the solution on the impossible road that brought him to his sixth title. As the season gets underway Rossi shows no signs of holding back on his increasingly competitive Yamaha. Yet despite spending much of his time chasing king of the track Honda, Valentino actually finds an ally in his ex-bosses who, too full of themselves, think they can sink him with a rider that, while good, is by no means a champion. Alex Barros is called to play the role of lead rider at Honda, something he is not accustomed to doing. Max Biaggi would have been better, or best of all Sete Gibernau, who incredibly and unexpectedly grew in stature and showed that he was capable of challenging the champion on level terms.

The Spaniard is helped by a piece of luck in the second race of the season at Jerez. Valentino sets a furious pace in testing, giving the impression that he will make short work of winning his second race in a row. But in the morning the rain sets in and the Yamaha, which has never been tested in the wet, is not yet ready for those conditions. Rossi tries all the same, but, struggling to control the bike, quickly realises that it will not be his day. He fails to finish on the podium, a fate that also befalls him in the next race at Le Mans in France. Rossi never liked the French track, but that takes nothing away from the Spaniard, who fully deserves his victory. Rossi fails to master his Yamaha, which is traditionally strong at Le Mans, where his team-mate Carlos Checa finishes second, the best performance of his season and his only podium finish.

Valentino has to bow before Biaggi in France. He had not failed to finish on the podium for two races in a row since his debut in 500, back in 2000. Furthermore, he slipped out of the lead of the world championship for two consecutive races. Something needed to be done.

His home track of Mugello proves a godsend, even though

v.2k+04
sprockets
chains
www.vaz.com.b
GAULOISES
YAMAHA
GAULOISES
DAINESE
GAULOISES
YAMAHA
MOTUL
MICHELIN

YAMAHA HAS TAKEN A BEATING FROM HONDA FOR THE LAST 12 YEARS. NOW THEY'VE BEEN REMINDED OF WHAT VICTORY TASTES LIKE

I OFTEN MAKE THE DIFFERENCE

Gibernau seems to have prepared a trap for him. Valentino understands straightaway. Conceding Rossi a victory, in front of his own fans, would give him too much of a boost, so the Spaniard sticks close to him, fighting tooth and nail until the rain comes down and washes away his efforts. The race is then fought over six final laps on a damp track, where those who have nothing to lose (Troy Bayliss, Norick Abe and Ruven Xaus, for example) fight their own battles, ignoring the fact that the leaders are vying for an important slice of the championship. But Rossi's hunger for victory makes the difference, and he gets the win.

There is a re-match seven days later in the Spaniard's home GP. The same protagonists, this time without the rain, serve up a similar result. A hat-trick of wins is within Rossi's grasp at the track known as the University of Motorbiking: Assen. The circuit normally stages very good races, but just occasionally it serves up a classic. This race was one such, fought tooth and nail for every tiny advantage. On the very last lap Sete's front mudguard brushes against Valentino's rear tyre. It is the lightest of touches but it spells victory for the Italian and defeat for the chasing Spaniard. There is a note of controversy afterwards at the press conference as Gibernau responds to a loaded question by saying somewhat mockingly: 'If Valentino says he had a problem with his brakes, I believe him.'

IT WAS A PLEASURE TO RACE LIKE THAT.
I WOULD HAVE LIKED ANOTHER TWO OR THREE LAPS

BRITISH GP

CELEBRATING WITH EDWARDS AT DONINGTON

CAPIROSSI-BIAGGI CONTROVERSY AT ESTORIL. MAX FAILS TO AVOID COLLISIO

NOW I MUSTN'T LOSE MY HEAD.
I JUST NEED TO KEEP RIDING
MY OWN RACE

PORTUGUESE GP

TH CAPIROSSI'S DUCATI AND LORIS FALLS OFF. THE ROMAN'S RACE AND CHAMPIONSHIP-WINNING CHANCES END HERE. ROSSI WINS HIS SIXTH TITLE

THE CHAMPIONSHIP DISCOVERS THE DESERT WITH THE FIRST EVER RACE IN QATAR: NOT MANY FANS AND TWO BODYGUARDS FOR ROSSI

agv
TRIBU DEI CHIHUAHUA
GAULOISES
YAMAHA
46
GAULOISES
GAULOISES
YAMAHA
YAMAHA

SSI'S ANSWER COMES IN MALAYSIA. HE DOMINATES THE RACE, WHILE GIBERNAU IS 7th, 21.8 SECONDS BEHIND. HE IS SARCASTIC ABOUT THE SPANIARD: 'FROM MY POINT OF VIEW HE RODE A PERFECT RACE'

Rossi flies towards a target that no longer seems just a dream. The Spaniard puts up tough opposition, but he can be tamed. Rio is next and Sete shows in testing that he is on great form. When the race gets underway he proves too eager, falling off in the first few laps, while Valentino's difficulties in testing are repeated in the race.

But seeing his opponent on the ground does not stop him from pushing back his own boundaries. 'I understood I just had to make do with this bike.' This does not come naturally to him, but you need to have fallen off to understand – something he does soon after.

The Sachsenring kartdrome awaits, as does Max Biaggi, who is in awesome form in testing and also in the race. Valentino struggles with the bike and tyres and is forced to be patient. When Gibernau quickly falls off, the world championship dream is on again, though he misses his chance to show the big bosses of Honda what they had let slip through their fingers by failing to stop three Hondas from making the podium. But Rossi cannot be too unhappy, as he is beginning to close in on the title with their main rivals.

From that moment on, the man from Tavullia makes no mistakes. He dominates at Donington with only a little concern about the heavy clouds on the horizon, but this time the weather plays by the rules. He keeps Gibernau at bay at Brno, which is always a delicate race, with Honda playing its trump card. It gives its official bike to Sete and Biaggi too: Max immediately adopts it, but does worse than with the 'satellite', though the Spaniard shows that he knows all the bike's secrets and dominates the race.

Rossi the strategist shows all his insight for the tactical

VISION
mistral VISION
300 736 826
105
motogp

side of racing. Nobody can stand up to him in Portugal and he takes the win after overwhelming the opposition. Loris Capirossi could have caused him a few problems – the rider was on top form and his Ducati was improving.

But Biaggi hits him on the first lap and his chase from the rear sees him finish halfway back in the field. The Gibernau threat is tempered by bike problems, and Makoto Tamada and the Bridgestone tyres would only become a problem at Motegi, the race Rossi fears the most. He plans a great offensive on Honda at the track owned by the Japanese manufacturer. Tohru Ukawa, Vale's team-mate in his first season of MotoGP, lies in ambush, but the only big obstacle is the Bridgestone tyres and Tamada. The likeable Japanese wins the race, but Rossi remains fully in control of the world championship.

Too much so, some would say. The trap awaits in the pit lane at Qatar. Valentino, or rather his team, is to blame. Australian chief engineer Jeremy Burgess and his men make a schoolboy error by going onto the track on scooters and laying down rubber on the starting grid. The reaction (even by those not directly involved) verges on the hysterical. Valentino, who is already unhappy with the very slippery desert track, finds himself relegated from the third row of the grid to 21st, behind the rest of the field.

His race is compromised anyway (it later emerges that other Yamaha riders have problems with fuel supply), but Valentino throws himself body and soul into a fantastic comeback, finishing fourth. He then drops his concentration for a second and ends up flying off. 'I could see my glove was all bloodied and thought that my hand had swollen up.' His finger is a bit the worst for wear, and he explodes in anger –

216

THE AUSTRALIAN TRACK SEEMS LIKE A ROAD IN TAVULLIA. ROSSI'S FANS INVADE THE CIRCUIT AND CELEBRATE WITH THEIR CHAMPI

HAT A SHOW' IS THE SLOGAN ON THE T-SHIRT DESCRIBING THE RIDER'S FANTASTIC 2004 SEASON

TO BEAT ME HONDA HAS TO BUY ME

AUSTRALIAN GP

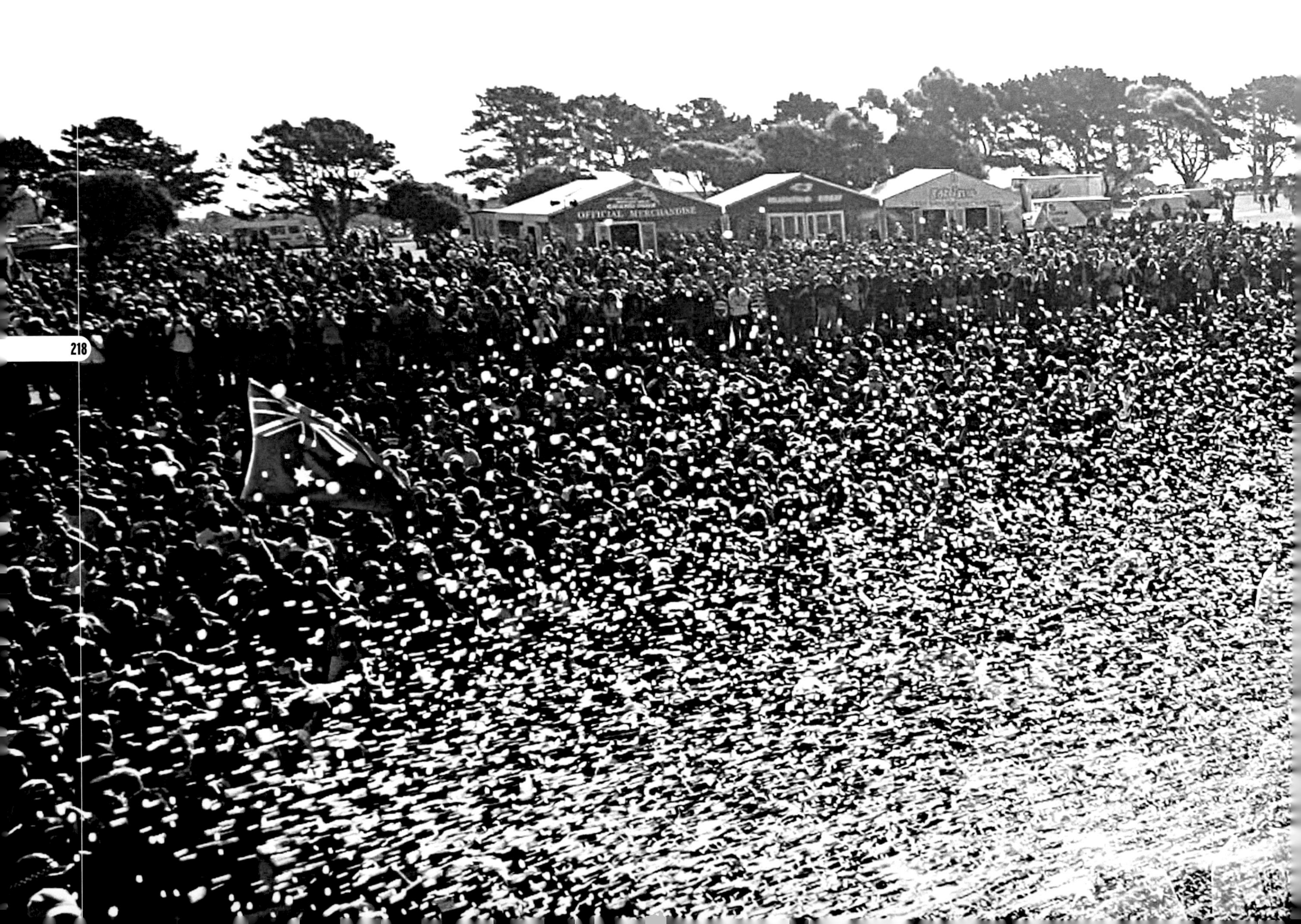

MICHELIN
CHE

MICHELIN

LENTINO ROSSI'S TRIUMPH: 'I BELIEVED I'D WIN THE TITLE, BUT NOT SO QUICKLY. I THOUGHT IT WOULD TAKE TWO YEARS.' HE THEN PRAISES GIBERNAU: 'I'VE NEVER HAD A RIVAL LIKE HIM'

anger directed against the system, but also against Sete Gibernau, his one-time friend, who he now saw as an opportunistic traitor. Rossi then turns his guns on chief engineer Juan Martinez, who worked on the suspensions of his bike when with Honda: 'I helped him make a name for himself and now he is spying on me,' claims the champion.

Still seething with rage, he arrives in Malaysia for the next race meet like a coiled spring. The first salvo is fired in the pre-race press conference, where he piles insult after insult onto the Spaniard without looking him in the eye. He repeats his psychological domination of his opponent in the race, which he wins emphatically in front of a brilliant Biaggi. Gibernau is left to drown in his own anger.

Valentino's title bid is now gathering steam, with the stage set for his coronation in Australia. However, Gibernau is not ready to concede defeat just yet and pushes Rossi all the way to the line with a gritty display. The Spaniard does all he can to ruin Vale's party, but with a breathtaking last lap, where he has everything to lose, Rossi passes his rival one last time to secure the win and a sixth world title. What a show! There is one last chapter to this season, with a win in front of 120,000 fans in Valencia, in Gibernau's home GP. With nine wins, just like with the fantastic Honda, Valentino Rossi proves once and for all that the rider is more important than the bike.

VALENTINO AND YAMAHA: A HISTORIC **DOUBLE**

HAVING RAISED EYEBROWS WITH YAMAHA IN 2004, HE'S OFF AGAIN

Winning everything was not enough. He took the 125cc title, then the 250, then the last ever edition of the 500, the first MotoGP Championship and then the second. Then came the break-up with Honda and the move to Yamaha, switching to a bike that was seemingly past its best and out of contention. The goal was to take the Championship title in two years, yet he romped home in just one. What else could anyone possibly want from motorcycling? Most ordinary 25-year-olds who have everything start to find it a bit tedious: the clothes, the cars, the socialising, even the girls. But this is no ordinary 25-year-old. This is Valentino Rossi, a quite exceptional competitor, and a man with an addiction to winning. And the more he tastes victory, the more he wants to gorge himself. Vale thrives on a challenge – and on wiping the floor with his rivals.

DURING WINTER TESTING, MY TOUGHEST CHALLENGER WAS GIBERNAU

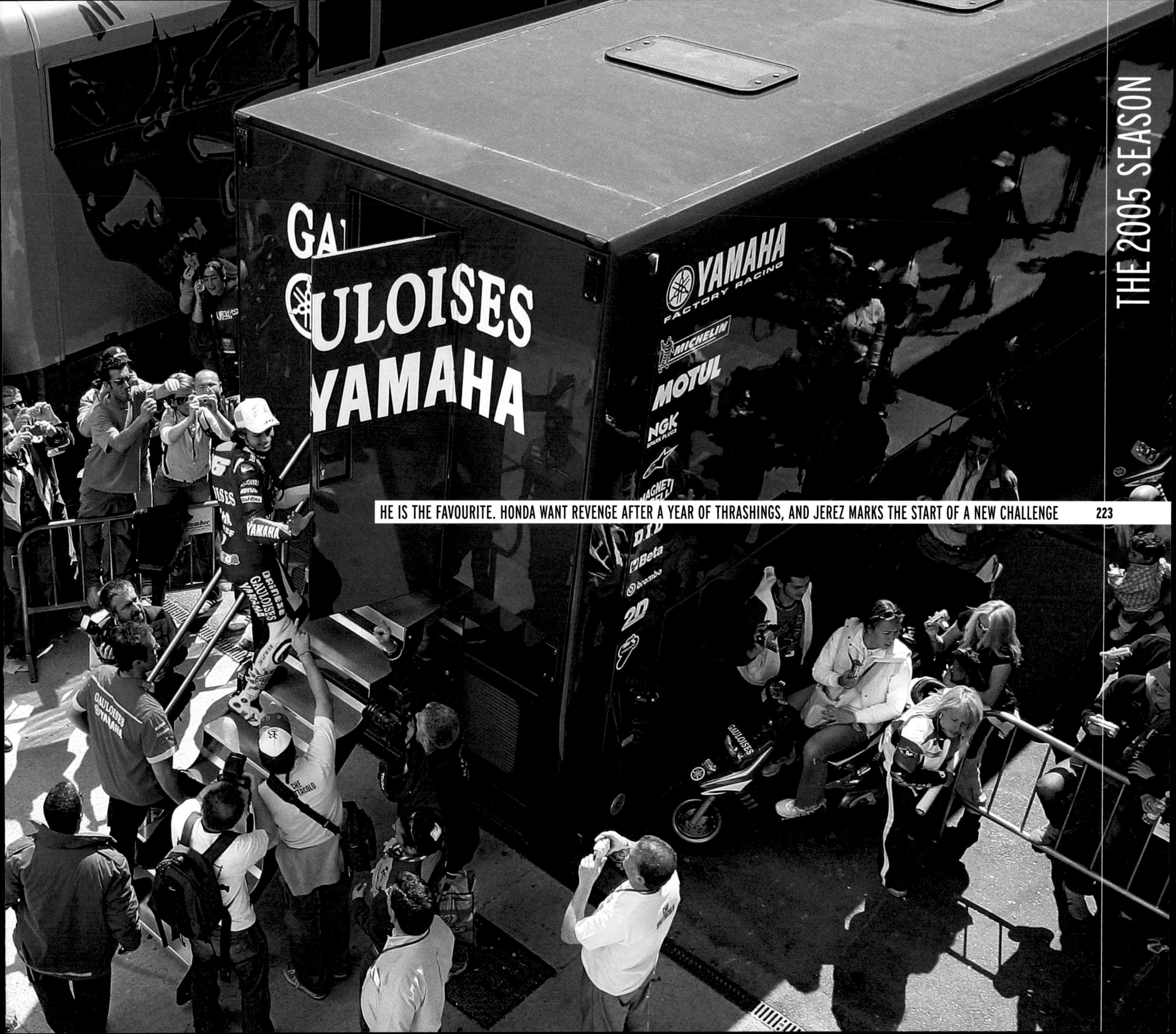

HE IS THE FAVOURITE. HONDA WANT REVENGE AFTER A YEAR OF THRASHINGS, AND JEREZ MARKS THE START OF A NEW CHALLENGE

THE HONDA HAS DISTINCTLY QUICKER ACCELERATION: OURS IS A BIKE FOR REAL MEN

SPANISH GP

He thrives on that unique feeling of invincibility, a sensation only partly explained by the insuperable machine he sits astride. The real beauty of it is pushing the limits, even if in the cold light of day you would rather the boundaries did not exist. Valentino had expected 2005 to be reasonably difficult. He had already done more than enough by riding the Yamaha to victory the previous year. A big step, because as Rossi had rapidly discovered, the Iwata engineers were no mugs. It was not the bike that was to blame for them constantly trailing their rivals. Before he arrived, the M1 may not have been the world's fastest bike, but that was only because its riders did not know how to bring the best out of it, and the fact that they were competing with another top-class bike ridden by . . . Valentino Rossi. It was on a hiding to nothing. Now, though, things were different. 'Il Fenomeno' was on Yamaha's side. Perhaps now it would be possible to take a breather, relatively speaking. However, things did not work out that way.

Everyone was at least partly to blame: the engineers, the team and even the rider. Instead of making progress during the winter, there were nothing but setbacks. The team were trying too hard. The new M1 had been designed according to the specifications of Rossi and Jeremy Burgess, his chief mechanic, whom he brought with him from Honda. It seemed an improvement on the previous year, but was not good enough to hold off the champion's ever-more-competitive rivals.

'We made the mistake of trying to base its development on our impressions of the old bike. Instead, it was a completely different animal,' says the Italian at the time. The result is Rossi playing catch-up at the start of the season, a situation that only whets his competitive appetite. Honda, and in particular Sete Gibernau, are flying, but this does not stop Rossi wanting to give it a go, even when victory seems impossible.

 INAUGURAL GP IN THE RAIN, CHINA'S GAIN – OR RATHER ROSSI'S. SHANGHAI MARKS HIS SECOND WIN IN THREE, AND A GAP IS ALREADY STARTING TO OPEN UP OVER HIS RIVALS. FRENCHMAN OLIVIER JACQ

AKES A SURPRISE SECOND PLACE

MERCILESS ROSSI FREEZES OUT GIBERNAU, FINISHING IN FRON

-FTER A NAIL-BITING LAST LAP. THE SPANIARD MUST SETTLE FOR SECOND, THREE TENTHS OF A SECOND BEHIND

Just like in the memorable and much-debated battle of Jerez, which practically ended the Championship before it had even begun, his rivals are ahead but still unable to take full advantage. Rossi seizes on this to heap pressure on his competitors, openly telling them: 'Take your chance now, because it's only a matter of time (until I'm back). We're starting to get the hang of the new bike and to solve some of its problems. And when we finally get there, it'll be tough for everyone else.' It is a message that only Alex Barros is willing, or fully able, to understand. In Portugal, straight after Spain, Rossi is struggling, while Gibernau is once again going great guns. Sete is leading, with the race his for the taking. The Brazilian is in second place, with Valentino still hanging in there, but still a long way back. The conditions are damp, which make things difficult enough, but then the heavens open, greasing the bend at the end of the home straight (320km/h down to 80km/h), where the first to fall . . . is the race leader. A mistake is a mistake, whatever the circumstances, and so while the Italian champion is enjoying a second place finish that sets him up nicely for the rest of the season, it is looking more and more like mission impossible for the Spaniard. And then comes the inaugural Chinese Grand Prix, which brings motorbike racing to the potentially lucrative Chinese market for the first time. Off the track, everything is new and exciting, but the race itself proves a bit of a letdown. The track has been designed with cars in mind, and MotoGP is following hot on the heels of Formula One. Valentino once again lets everyone know that his team are still struggling, telling reporters: 'Here, the best thing we can do is to hold on for a place.' During practice, everyone else is flying, but then on the Sunday morning Rossi gets what proves to be a lucky break when a downpour leaves the track drenched.

VALENTINO RECEIVING AN HONORARY DEGREE IN COMMUNICATION FROM THE UNIVERSITY OF URBINO.

I COMMUNICATE THROUGH SYMBOLS, COLOURS AND NUMBERS

E DOCTOR IS CONGRATULATED BY GIOVANNI BOGLIOLO, RECTOR OF THE UNIVERSITY. THE FACULTY'S GREAT HALL IS FILLED WITH CHEERING FANS

AT MUGELLO, WEARING HIS GRADUATION HELMET. A HISTORIC TRIUMPH OVER BIAGGI, CAPIROSSI AND MELANDRI.

A VICTORY WITH TOP HONOURS

ITALIAN GP

While the Spaniard never looks like getting his head above water, at least partly because he is forced to use a set of tyres he was not happy with, the formerly rain-shy Rossi makes waves. Amid that Shanghai downpour, the Italian finds the perfect rear-end set-up for his bike, a development that will provide a platform for success over the rest of the season and dispel any lingering fears he may have. He literally flies round the course, particularly during a dream first lap, when he overtakes his rivals in bunches.

The Yamaha ace is going full speed while the others – apart from Kenny Roberts, who is later forced to retire due to bike troubles – are slowing down. More than a mere victory, this is an overwhelming triumph from the supposedly struggling Rossi that leaves his in-form opponents searching for excuses. Though the season has just begun, a chasm is opening up between the champion and the pretenders to his crown – so much so that people were already calculating when the season would be mathematically over. Rossi is racing against himself. As Marco Melandrini, a former friend and now a rival, wisecracked in Barcelona, 'This World Championship is between Valentino and Rossi.' It sounded like a joke, but it was in fact an unconditional surrender; no one even came close to matching him over the course of that season.

Occasionally, someone would get the better of him in a race, as happened in the United States, when Grand Prix Motorcycle Racing finally returned to the Promised Land. The circuit, risky for 500cc bikes in the 1990s, was now plainly hazardous for MotoGP, in spite of repeated overhauls. The track contained innumerable small traps, and the home riders, Nicki Hayden and Colin Edwards, were invincible, if just for one weekend.

It is not very often that someone finishes ahead of

Alice Alice Alice Alice Alice Alice
REPSOL
DUCATI
GAULOISES YAMAHA
Alice

ROWDS, COLOUR AND BIAGGI ON FORM. THE MUGELLO GP WAS AN ALL-ITALIAN AFFAIR, WITH ROSSI IN FRONT AS USUAL

Valentino Rossi, but when two people do it in the same race, as happened at that year's US Grand Prix, then it is certainly big news. To commemorate Yamaha's fiftieth anniversary, the Yamaha Factory Team deck the bike out in traditional yellow and black US racing colours, with Rossi wearing yellow gloves to match. The house of Iwata hail the US Grand Prix as the event of the year, spending huge amounts of money and acting as if victory was theirs before the engines were even switched on. Rossi shies away from the pre-race hype, but still rides to his worst result of the season, narrowly missing out on second place when he decides against an all-out attack on (his team-mate) Edwards on the last bend. The risks of completely ruining the Yamaha party are simply too great. Nicky Hayden and the official Honda team have already put a dampener on the occasion by winning their first race in 23 attempts after almost an 18-month wait. In fact, it is the first time a Honda has finished in pole position since Rossi left – a result that would not be repeated that season.

From then on in the champion waltzes to his seventh crown in style, the only blip occurring at his unlucky Motegi circuit. Early on in the season he had to draw on all his reserves, from showing true grit at Jerez to demonstrating great nerve for his flying victory in the rain in Shanghai. Then came the real turning point, in France, where his Yamaha finally starts to ride as he had hoped. It is there that the champion begins to realise he can beat anyone, even Sete Gibernau, whom he left in his slipstream on the last bend thanks to a combination of his formidable new Michelins and extraordinary skill. The result speaks for itself, and his new-found confidence means he will be on a high going into the one Grand Prix he wanted to win more than any other: Mugello. Having Capirossi and the Ducati team on the podium with him at the French GP only

AN AGGRESSIVE RIDE BRINGS VALENTINO A SEVENTH MONTMELÒ VICTORY. HIS FINAL TIME IS 47 SECONDS QUICKER THAN IN 2004

GRAN PREMI
2005
11 Checa
12 Capirossi
13 Checa
14 Rolfo
GAULOISES
movistar
HONDA
Telefonica
Castrol
BLACK PRINCE
domino
YAMAHA

 THE YELLOW YAMAHA STYLE AT LAGUNA SECA: HELMET, RACING SUIT AND BIKE. A WINNING LOOK

BELOW, THE US RIDERS CELEBRATE. HAYDEN AND EDWARDS LEAVE SUPER-VALENTINO BEHIND

 PHENOMENAL ACROBATICS ON A SOAKING WET TRACK. AT DONINGTON VALE TRIUMPHS OVER HIS MOST FEARED ADVERSARY: THE RAIN. THEN MIMICS PLAYING THE VIOLIN AS HE CROSSES THE LINE. APPLAU

OM WET-WEATHER SPECIALISTS KENNY ROBERTS AND ALEX BARROS ON THE PODIUM

RARE IMAGES: VALENTINO ON THE GRAVEL DURING TESTING AT SACHSENRING. THE RACE IS A DIFFERENT STORY: HIS 50TH VICTORY IN 90 PREMIER CLASS RACES TAKES HIM 120 POINTS AHEAD OF MELANDE

I WAS LUCKY: HERE SETE WAS QUICKER

GERMAN GP

serves to whet his appetite for the big one. On the podium, 'The Doctor' appears as a real doctor, wearing a graduation cap, with his honorary degree on display. Just a few days earlier, the Carlo Bo University in Urbino (where Rossi was born, on 16 February 1979), had conferred an honorary degree in Communication Science on the Italian ace in recognition of his sporting achievements. It was an emotional moment – even for a young man accustomed to thrills – and one that was particularly satisfying for his mother Stefania, who had wanted her son to be an architect but had to bow to the inevitable when he left school to take up racing full time. It provided a memorable diversion in a season of non-stop action. Next up is Barcelona, home of one of his fiercest rivals Sete Gibernau, who cracks late in the race, and not for the first or last time either. Then comes the Netherlands, where the victim of Rossi's merciless driving is Marco Melandri, who on this occasion manages to stay close to his friend and rival right to the end. And then on to the UK, where in terrible riding conditions his nearest challengers, Kenny Roberts and Alex Barros, are happy with a place on the podium.

The German Grand Prix at Sachsenring is a defining moment for a number of reasons. It is not one of Rossi's favourite venues, but the race comes right before the mid-season break, so a good finish there means a relaxing month's holiday. Gibernau, who had inflicted on Rossi one of the most disappointing defeats of his career when he beat him in 2003 – although to be fair, a lot was down to Rossi's mistake on the last bend – is back on form and going well. So well, in fact, that he leads going into the last bend, only to miscalculate at the first braking marker, allowing Valentino the simple task of sweeping past him for his 10th win from 12 consecutive races.

GAULOISES
GAULOISES
GAULOISES
4

ROSSI AND MELANDRI TAKE A TUMBLE. THEIR RACE ENDS ON THE 12TH LAP. MARCO IS HIT BY VALE'S M1 AND INJURES HIS RIGHT FOOT

ROSSI WINS HIS 7TH TITLE IN SEPANG. IN THE RACE, HOWEVER, HE IS SECOND TO AN ON-FORM LORIS CAPIROSSI, UNCATCHABLE ON THE DUCATI AND THE NEW BRIDGESTONE TYRES. ONLY IN 1997, AT BRN

D VALE SECURED THE TITLE (125) WITHOUT ALSO WINNING THE RACE

The win also means an enjoyable summer and, more importantly, the near certainty of a very early championship victory. When racing starts again, at Brno, it throws up more of the same. Sete is there again, but this time does not even have the consolation of a second-place finish. Vale overtakes him with a few laps to go, and then the Honda runs out of juice not far from the line.

By then it is calculations time. The end of the season seems miles away, but the finishing line tantalisingly close. Motegi is the worst possible place for a party, which should have served as a warning. 'I told my friends not to come, but they wouldn't listen,' joked Valentino later, when the crown was in the bag. But there was nothing to laugh about in Japan. The track there, a typical stop-and-go course, with none of those fast bends on which he likes to impress his fans, is not one of his favourites. The others are flying, among them Loris Capirossi who seems back to his old self. Despite a poor performance in qualifying, Rossi gives it a go. After all, unless Max Biaggi could come up with an unlikely victory, a podium finish would have secured the title. On paper it looks easy, but in the event Rossi is a long way off his minimum objective of third place, meaning there is no podium place and no party on this occasion.

Sometimes, even the mighty Valentino Rossi has a bad day, and the Japanese GP ends with him and his friend Marco Melandri on the gravel, the latter with a gashed foot. Rossi is annoyed, but probably more for his friend's suffering than at the missed opportunity. The following week, he gets another chance to secure the title, this time in Malaysia, where he feels more at home. Sepang is a track full of beautiful memories where he already had countless victories, including a World Championship. More importantly, however, it is a place he enjoys driving. Now he wants to win in style, to exorcise the ghost of Japan, but is

DOUBLE CELEBRATION: CAPIROSSI WINS THE RACE, VALENTINO THE TITLE

up against a new and formidable adversary: Loris Capirossi's Bridgestone tyres, which are proving remarkably effective during the final laps of races. Rossi has to go for victory, of course, but resigns himself to second place when he realises that Loris was just 'toying' with him (as he put it) in the closing laps. Second on the podium guarantees him another title, with the celebrations really starting when Snow White and the Seven Dwarfs – one for each of his World Championships – are brought out to embrace their Prince. Although the job was finished, there were still another four races to be staged, almost a quarter of a championship, which can feel like an eternity when you are competing for pride alone. Still to come was Qatar, which Rossi remembered as having dirt on the track and being the scene of the so-called 'dirty trick' of arch-nemesis Sete Gibernau, who reported Rossi to the authorities there after his mechanics wheel-spun a scooter to clean his grid position. The penalty was harsh but non-negotiable, and the champion had to start from the back of the grid, from where he made his way into fourth place before a lapse in concentration caused him to fall and scrape his finger on the asphalt. In addition to the previous year's bad experience, the newly crowned champion's Yamaha had now been out of sorts for a couple of weeks and had inferior tyres. However, all of this is put behind him in a majestic three-way battle with Gibernau and Melandri from which he emerges, not altogether surprisingly, victorious and grinning broadly. Speaking straight after the race, while still sweating from his exertions, the champion describes it as, 'The best race of the year, the best way to celebrate.' Not even close friends or beautiful women could top that for Rossi; the man knows no other way.

97
99
01
02
99
YAMAHA
46

HE TITLE GAG: VALE WITH SNOW WHITE AND THE SEVEN DWARFS. MEANWHILE, IN TAVULLIA THE PARTY IS ON. LOTS OF YELLOW AND THEIR NUMBER ONE CITIZEN'S NUMBER 46

1997
125

SMALL BUT **TOUGH**

ENGINE
Single cylinder 2-stroke, liquid-cooled, rotary disc. Displacement: 124.8cc.

POWER
Over 47 bhp at 12,700 rpm. Bore and stroke: 54 x 54.5 mm.

FRAME
Aluminium sloping twin-spar.

DIMENSIONS
Tank capacity: 14 litres. Weight: 71 kg. Wheelbase: 1,270 mm.

FRONT BRAKE
Single 273 mm carbon disc, variable diameter 4-piston calliper.

APRILIA **RS 125 R**

WHEELS
Magnesium alloy, 17" front and rear.
Dunlop tyres.

SUSPENSION
Double adjustment 38/35 mm upside down hydraulic WP forks.

GEARBOX
Entirely removable 6-speed gearbox.
Dry multiplate clutch.

REAR BRAKE
Single 172 mm steel disc.
Opposing twin piston callipers.

ROSSI'S APRILIA 125, ON WHICH HE WON HIS FIRST WORLD TITLE, SPORTS THE UNMISTAKEABLE YELLOW NO. 46 ON A BLUE BACKGROUND. NOALE'S RS COMPLEMENTS VALE'S DRIVING SKILLS: THEY ARE A

L-ITALIAN DAVID THAT TRIUMPH OVER THE HONDA GOLIATH, WINNING 11 OUT OF 15 RACES AND DOMINATING THE CHAMPIONSHIP. THE PARTNERSHIP WILL GO ON TO TAKE THE 250 CROWN AS WELL

1999
250

ITALIAN PHENOMENON

ENGINE
Liquid cooled, rotary disc 90° V2 2-stroke.

POWER
Over 96 bhp at 12,500 rpm. Bore and stroke: 54 x 54.5 mm.

FRAME
Aluminium sloping twin-spar.

DIMENSIONS
Tank capacity: 23 litres. Weight: 96 kg. Wheelbase: 1,270 mm. Length: 1,970 mm.

FRONT BRAKE
Twin 255/273 mm carbon disc.

APRILIA **RSW 250**

WHEELS
Carbon, 17" front and rear.
Dunlop tyres.

SUSPENSION
Double adjustment 42 mm upside down hydraulic Öhlins forks.

GEARBOX
Entirely removable 6-speed gearbox.
Dry multiplate clutch.

REAR BRAKE
Single 190 mm steel disc.

ROSSI'S APRILIA 250, ON WHICH HE WON HIS SECOND WORLD TITLE. IN 1999 VALE WINS 9 RACES ON THE RSW. IN THESE PHOTOS, THE MUGELLO ITALIAN GP BIKE, EASILY RECOGNISABLE THANKS TO ITS PEA

LOVE DESIGN. ON THE TRACK, HOWEVER, ROSSI RIDES LIKE A TRUE WARRIOR. THEN HONDA COME KNOCKING

2001
500

TOKYO **YELLOW**

ENGINE
499cc 112° V4 2-stroke. Reed valve admission in the crankcase. Single drive shaft.

POWER
Some 190 bhp at 13,000 rpm. Bore and stroke: 54 x 54.4 mm.

FRAME
Aluminium sloping twin-spar with aluminium swing arm.

DIMENSIONS
Weight: 131 kg.
Wheelbase: 1,400 mm.
Length: 2,010 mm.

FRONT BRAKE
Twin 290/320 mm carbon discs, two 4-piston callipers.

HONDA **NSR 500**

WHEELS
Magnesium rims, 17" front,
17"-16.5" rear.
Michelin tyres.

SUSPENSION
46 mm upside down Showa forks.

GEARBOX
6-speed.
Dry multiplate clutch.

REAR BRAKE
Single 200 mm twin piston steel disc.

 VALENTINO ROSSI'S HONDA NSR ENDS THE 500 ERA ON TOP. HAVING BEEN ROSSIFUMI IN 125CC AND VALENTINIK IN 250, THE NEW NICKNAME, THE DOCTOR, APPEARS IN 2001. 'IN ITALY, EVERYONE I

CTOR, EVEN IF THEY'VE NEVER STUDIED. I COULD BE A DOCTOR OF RACING AND THAT'S DEFINITELY NO BAD THING'

2002 MOTOGP

THE **INVINCIBLE**

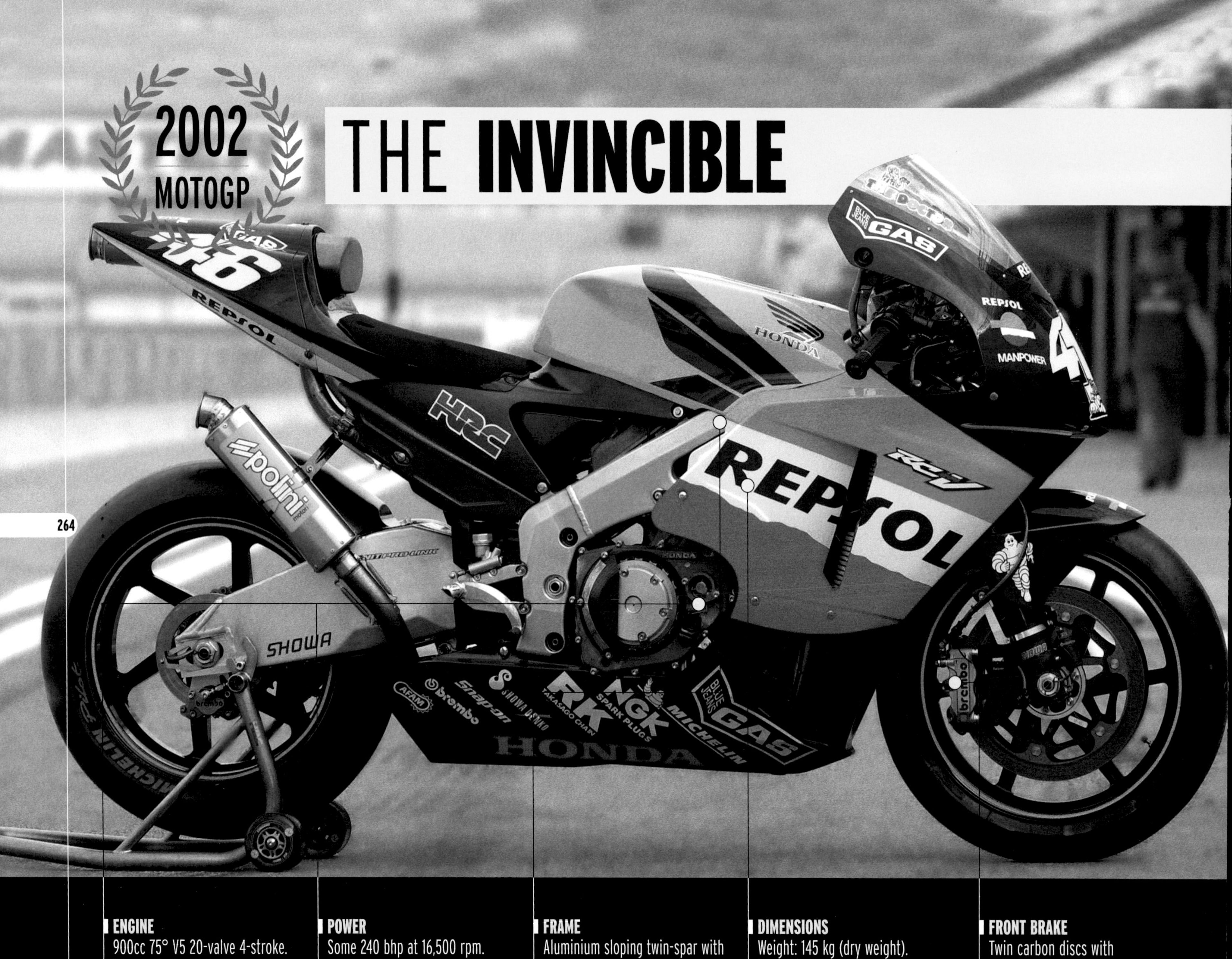

ENGINE
900cc 75° V5 20-valve 4-stroke. Electronic fuel injection.

POWER
Some 240 bhp at 16,500 rpm.

FRAME
Aluminium sloping twin-spar with aluminium swing arm.

DIMENSIONS
Weight: 145 kg (dry weight).
Wheelbase: 1,440 mm.
Length: 2,050 mm.
Width: 600 mm.

FRONT BRAKE
Twin carbon discs with radially mounted callipers.

HONDA **RC211V**

WHEELS
17" front, 16.5" rear.
Magnesium rims.
Michelin tyres.

SUSPENSION
Upside down front forks.
Pro-link rear suspension system.

GEARBOX
6-speed. Dry multiplate clutch.

REAR BRAKE
Single steel disc with twin piston calliper.

THE HONDA RC211V DOMINATES THE FIRST SEASON OF THE 4-STROKE ERA. THE BIKE WINS 14 RACES OUT OF 16: 11 WITH VALENTINO ROSSI, 2 WITH ALEX BARROS AND ONE WITH TOHRU UKAWA. AMIDST A

E JAPANESE TECHNOLOGY ARE THE ULTRA-ITALIAN BREMBO BRAKES. THE MAN ASTRIDE THE 240 BHP BEAST IS ALSO ITALIAN: HIS NAME IS VALENTINO ROSSI

2003

MOTOGP

RECORD BREAKER

ENGINE
900cc 75° V5 20-valve 4-stroke. Electronic fuel injection.

POWER
Some 240 bhp at 16,500 rpm.

FRAME
Aluminium sloping twin-spar with aluminium swing arm.

DIMENSIONS
Weight: 145 kg (dry weight).
Wheelbase: 1,440 mm.
Length: 2,050 mm.
Width: 600 mm.

FRONT BRAKE
Twin carbon discs with radially mounted callipers.

HONDA **RC211V**

WHEELS
17" front, 16.5" rear.
Magnesium rims.
Michelin tyres.

SUSPENSION
Upside down front forks.
Pro-link rear suspension system.

GEARBOX
6-speed.
Dry multiplate clutch.

REAR BRAKE
Single steel disc with twin piston calliper.

 A CHAMPIONSHIP DOMINATED BY ROSSI AND THE RC211V. THE DOCTOR WINS 9 RACES, GIBERNAU 4 AND BIAGGI 2: A TOTAL OF 15 OUT OF 16 FOR HONDA. THE OTHER RACE GOES TO CAPIROSSI'S DUCA

EVER IN RECENT CHAMPIONSHIP HISTORY HAS ONE BIKE SO COMPLETELY HELD SWAY. BUT VALE IS ABOUT TO PROVE THE IMPORTANCE OF THE RIDER BY SWITCHING TO YAMAHA

2004
MOTOGP

REVENGE

ENGINE
990cc 16-valve inline four. Magneti Marelli electronics.

POWER
Some 230 bhp at 16,500 rpm.

FRAME
Aluminium sloping twin-spar with aluminium swing arm.

WEIGHT
149 kg (dry weight). Tank capacity: 22 litres.

FRONT BRAKE
Twin 320 mm carbon discs.

YAMAHA **M1**

WHEELS
16.5" front and rear.
Magnesium rims.
Michelin tyres.

SUSPENSION
Öhlins front and rear.

GEARBOX
6-speed gearbox.
Dry multiplate clutch.

REAR BRAKE
Single 220 mm steel disc.

THE RESPONSE IS NOT LONG IN COMING. THE M1, A TOTAL FAILURE IN 2003, COMES BACK WITH A VENGEANCE AND WITH VALENTINO ON BOARD TAKES 9 VICTORIES, THE SAME NUMBER AS THE DOCTOR H

TALLED THE PREVIOUS SEASON ON BOARD THE HONDA RC211V. YAMAHA ARE BACK ON TOP, WINNING THEIR FIRST TITLE SINCE RAINEY'S IN 1992

2005 MOTOGP

SIMPLY THE BEST

ENGINE
990cc 16-valve inline four.
Magneti Marelli electronics.

POWER
Some 230 bhp at 16,500 rpm.

FRAME
Aluminium sloping twin-spar with longer aluminium swing arm than the 2004 model.

WEIGHT
149 kg (dry weight).
New-look tank with 22-litre capacity.

FRONT BRAKE
Twin 320 mm carbon discs.

YAMAHA **M1**

WHEELS
16.5" front and rear.
Magnesium rims.

SUSPENSION
Öhlins front and rear.

GEARBOX
6-speed gearbox.
Dry multiplate clutch.

REAR BRAKE
Single 220 mm steel disc.

VALENTINO IMMEDIATELY REPEATS HIS TRIUMPH AND YAMAHA WIN THE CONSTRUCTORS' CHAMPIONSHIP. THE M1 IS MUCH THE SAME AS IN 2004. A UNIQUE YELLOW VERSION IS RACED AT THE US G

HOMAGE TO THE KENNY ROBERTS ERA. EVEN GUIDO IS IN YELLOW, BUT HAYDEN WINS ON A HONDA AND SPOILS THE PARTY

SNAPSHOTS OF A PRODIGY

DAD GRAZIANO WITH VALENTINO AS A CHILD. VALE IS TALENTED ON ANY KIND OF TWO-WHEELER AND SHOWS OFF HIS TRICKS. PEDALLING NORMALLY WOULD BE TOO EASY

Mum Stefania, a surveyor for Tavullia council, wanted her son to go one step further than she had and become an architect or engineer. A glance at his report cards would have shown that this was no pipe dream. Stefania was the rational one in the family, while his father Graziano, a motorcycle racer himself, had a very different view of life. Once, at Imola, Stefania was supposed to take a photograph of him in action, but he did not even make it halfway round the track after almost inevitably coming off. She had long got over worrying during races.

Their marriage, the coming together of 'genius' and 'respectability' was unlikely to last, and so it proved. Valentino, however, was a successful amalgam of the two opposites. He was half sun and half moon, just as depicted on his helmets. However, in spite of being born with racing in his

Cognome ROSSI
Nome VALENTINO
nato il 16 FEBBRAIO 1979
(atto n. .... P. .... S. ....)
a URBINO (.......)
Cittadinanza ITALIANA
Residenza LONDRA
Via
Stato civile CELIBE
Professione PILOTA

CONNOTATI E CONTRASSEGNI SALIENTI
Statura 1,82 - 64 KG
Capelli BIONDI
Occhi AZZURRI
Segni particolari
46 - VINCENTE

Firma del titolare
IL SINDACO

TAVULLIA • PESARO •

 VALENTINO WITH MUM STEFANIA, AND BELOW, WITH HIS GUITAR. BUT HE DREAMS OF BIKES AND IN 1993, AT MISANO, THE 14-YEAR-OLD TRIES A GP BIKE. IT'S LOVE AT FIRST SIGHT

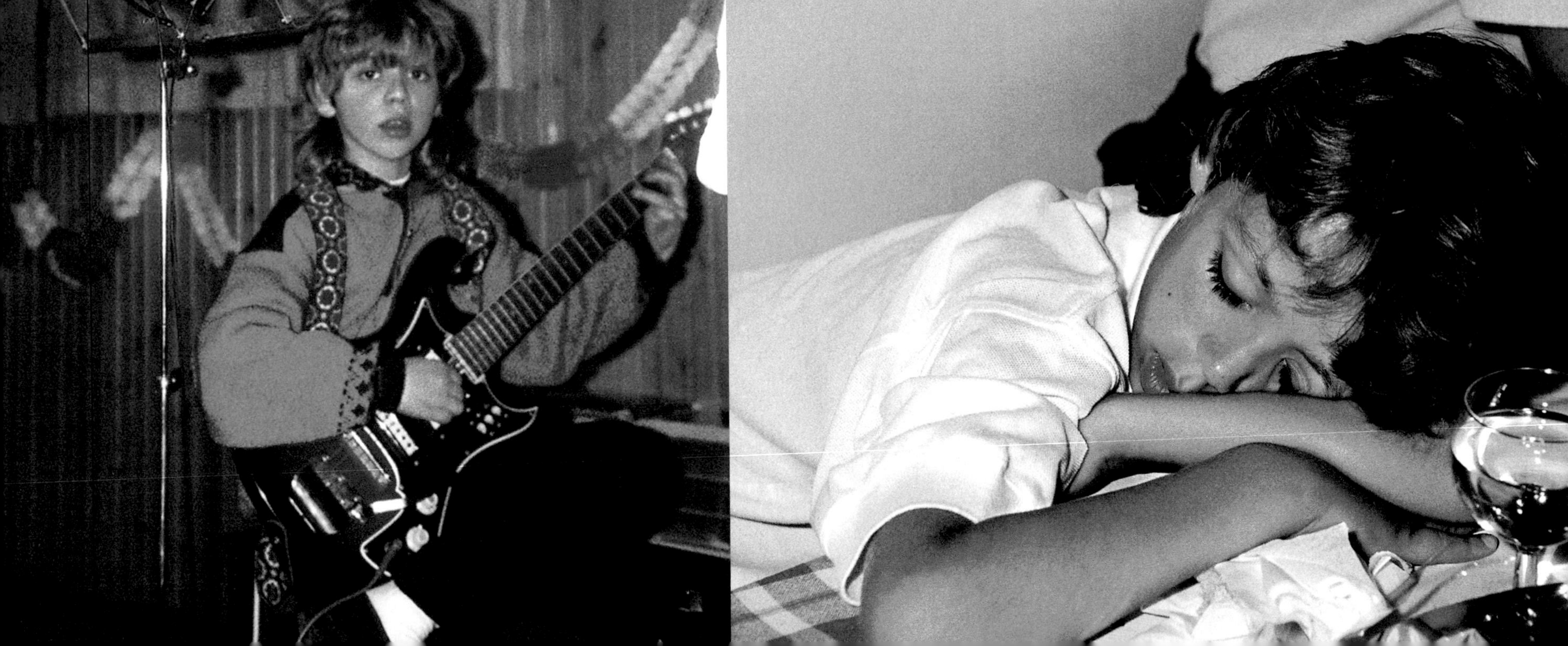

polini
UTAH
Marlboro
TEAM PILERI
HONDA
TEST
adige
polini
Marlboro
sèleco
diadora

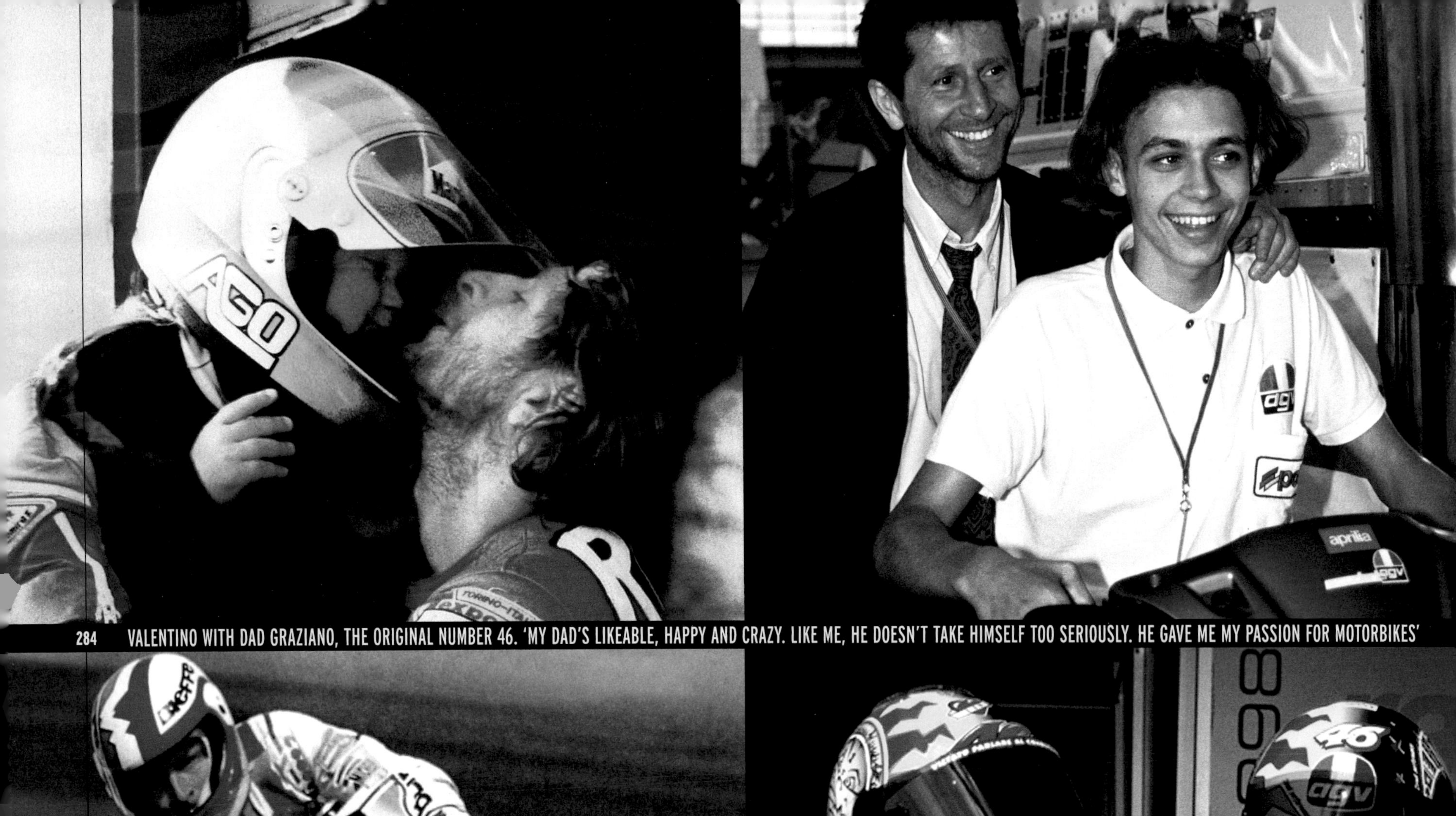

VALENTINO WITH DAD GRAZIANO, THE ORIGINAL NUMBER 46. 'MY DAD'S LIKEABLE, HAPPY AND CRAZY. LIKE ME, HE DOESN'T TAKE HIMSELF TOO SERIOUSLY. HE GAVE ME MY PASSION FOR MOTORBIKES'

46
Drudi Performance
arnette
agv
V. Rossi

BIEFFE
G. Rossi

LITTLE BROTHER LUCA LOVES MINIMOTO TOO. HE RACES WITH A 97 THAT 'MAGICALLY' BECOMES 46 WHEN TURNED UPSIDE DOWN. VALENTINO ALSO STARTED OUT RIDING MINIMOTO

CA LEARNS FROM THE MASTER AND GETS THE BEST SEAT

VALENTINO ALSO HONED HIS SKILLS ON GO-KARTS. HIS PRACTICE AREA HAS ALWAYS BEEN THE MYTHICAL QUARRY, RENAMED 'O'VAL(E)' IN HIS HONOUR. IT WAS HERE THAT ROSSI LEARNT TO SLI

blood, the youngster only found out about his father's riding successes much later from photographs and souvenirs.

Some of Valentino's earliest memories are of his father racing cars. For Graziano, this was a step down from motorcycles and, involving as it did several horrific crashes, brought him more pain than gain as a career. Vale, therefore, had racing in his blood and moved in racing circles. Among his father's friends were Marco Lucchinetti, Loris Reggiani and Virginio Ferrari, who discovered Valentino's talent for riding motorcycles.

Graziano wanted his son to race cars. He himself was by now a rally- and long-distance racing driver, and the young Vale was a successful Go-Karter. Unfortunately, racing karts was expensive and Graziano was not a man of means. This prompted the decision to focus on Minimoto, where Valentino was also going great guns. Ferrari, who were managing the Cagiva-Ducati team at the time, noticed the youngster's potential and got hold of a Cagiva 125 for him. It was the official bike of another former (125) racer, Claudio Lusuardi, complete with cigarette sponsorship markings, ironic in view of the fact that he did not smoke and would later 'declare war' on the tobacco industry.

Graziano's dream was becoming reality, while that of mum Stefania's was fading fast. Valentino's generation lived for and on their scooters. His group of friends become the scourge of Tavullia's local police, who chase them across the fields. Village life may have been short on entertainment, but proves perfect for building friendships. 'Uccio', Vale's classmate at junior school, who has followed the champion throughout his career, is in fact more of a brother than a friend, with Valentino even living in his house for a while. Albi, another friend from Tavullia, can even boast about the time he beat Rossi on a motorbike, in the Panoramica di Pesaro race. As well as the scooter, there was the Ape van, the love of his teenage years. Vale started driving it when his parents split up and he went to live in Montecchio, a neighbouring village. It may not have been the height of fashion, but it was essential for those trips to school on cold, wet winter mornings.

Reminiscing on his early days, Vale later said: 'The girls didn't look twice at us when we were in the Ape, but at least it kept us warm and we had a laugh.' The teenage exploits of Rossi and his friends meant frequent run-ins with the local police. Later, when he became world champion, Rossi would dedicate one of his victories to them, to make up for the trouble he had caused, but that day was still a long way off. In spite of a few good races in Minimoto and some good results in the Sport Production Championship, there are still very few signs of the prodigious talent that will later emerge.

N IMPORTANT ADDITION TO HIS ARRAY OF SKILLS AND PARTICULARLY SPECTACULAR WHEN USED WHILE RIDING ULTRA-POWERFUL 240 BHP GRAND PRIX MOTORCYCLES

ROSSI AND BEST FRIEND UCCIO, WHOSE DAD RINO (ABOVE LEFT) IS PRESIDENT OF THE FAN CLUB. 'UCCIO IS MY FRIEND EVEN THOUGH I'VE WON A FEW RACES AND BECOME WORLD CHAMPION. IT TAKES

ECIAL PERSON TO BUILD THE FRIENDSHIP WE HAVE.' ANOTHER GOOD FRIEND IS ALBI, THE ONLY ONE TO BEAT HIM ON A MOTORBIKE ROUND THE PANORAMICA DI PESARO

ABOVE: VALE WITH STEFANIA LUSUARDI. BELOW WITH GIAMPIERO SACCHI. RIGHT WITH ALESSIO CADALORA AND WALTER VILLA'S GRANDSON (ON THE BIKE) IN '93

36

VALENTINO GAINS EXPERIENCE WITH A CAGIVA MITO 125 STANDARD IN THE SPORT PRODUCTION CLASS IN '93. THEN, FOR THE FINALS, HE BECOMES PART OF CLAUDIO LUSUARDI'S OFFICIAL TEAM

RODE A FEW RACES ON A SANDRONI BEFORE SWITCHING TO APRILIA FOR THE EUROPEAN 125 CHAMPIONSHIP AND FINISHING ON THE PODIUM IN CADET CLASS

296 ROSSI'S FIRST PODIUM FINISH IN REAL RACING, AT MISANO, IN THE 1993 SPORT PRODUCTION FINAL. FROM POLE POSITION, HE FINISHED THIRD BEHIND WINNER ROBERTO LOCATELLI AND ANDREA BALLERIN

AUGUST 1996: UNFORGETTABLE FOR VALENTINO ROSSI. THE DAY HE TOOK HIS FIRST GP VICTORY AT BRNO, AHEAD OF MARTINEZ AND MANAKO ON AN APRILIA 125

40
invicta

SSI LIVES IN LONDON, 'A FANTASTIC CITY, APART FROM THE CLIMATE. I CAN LIVE THERE IN PEACE.'

At the time, these races were extremely popular. The grids were full of potential champions and getting to the front was no mean feat. Rossi won (twice, including one final), but was hardly something to write home about. After all, he rode the best bike, the Mito 125, for the official team and had all necessary support. 'In our part of the world,' Rossi explains, 'you'd say of a sound, reliable person, "he's a Mito, he's got that something extra".' The little Cagiva was, in fact, the only bike with 7 gears; all its competitors had 6.

Truth be told, the young Rossi is seen as privileged because of his surname, which is well-known in racing circles. Some people even suspect favouritism when Stefano Cruciani, a local lad who is challenging him for the title, is disqualified after taking victory in the last round of the Championship, after a collision with Valentino during the race.

Rossi's rise, however slow, is inexorable. Thanks to Fabrizio Guidotti's eye for spotting talent and Carlo Pernat's managerial skills, he becomes an Aprilia rider in 1995, competing in first the European and then the World Championships. Rossi is part of Mauro Noccioli's set-up for the European Championship, during which there are few high points. He does not win a single race, makes it on to the podium only six times, and finishes third overall.

It is more of the same when he makes his debut in the World Championship, with the same technical team, but under the management of Giampiero Sacchi.

There are a few flashes of brilliance, a few too many falls, but also a level of charisma rare in a 17-year-old. Here was a young man who took both life and racing by the horns. Rossi's first victory finally comes in the eleventh race, at Brno, a sign that the first seeds of stardom are sprouting. We would have

ROSSI'S FIRST VICTORY ON A 250, AT THE MAGICAL ASSEN CIRCUIT, MUST HOLD A SPECIAL PLACE IN HIS HEART. HERE HE IS CELEBRATING WITH THE GERMAN, FUCHS

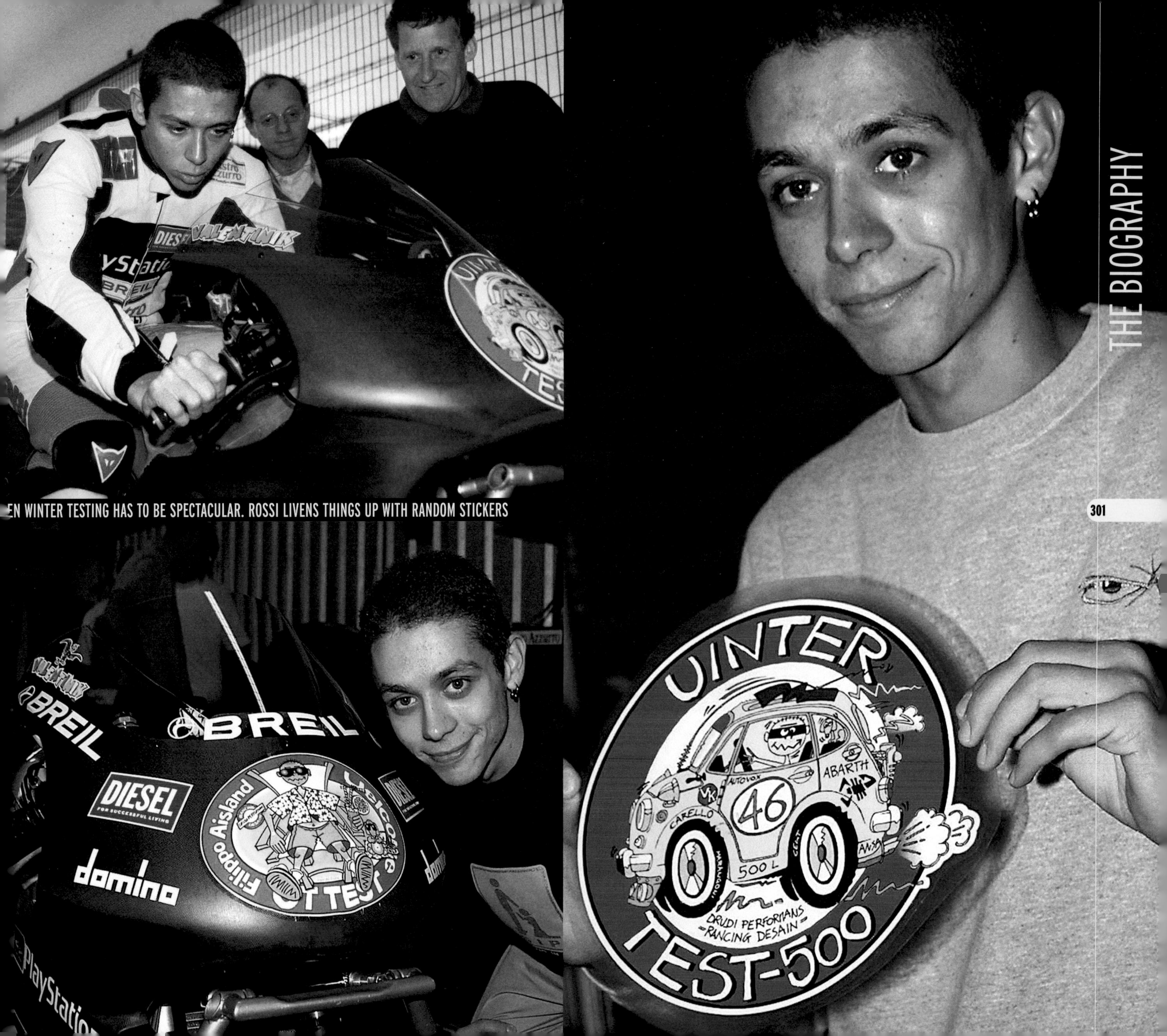

EN WINTER TESTING HAS TO BE SPECTACULAR. ROSSI LIVENS THINGS UP WITH RANDOM STICKERS

 ROSSI CHALKS UP HIS MAIDEN PREMIER CLASS VICTORY IN 2000 AT DONINGTON, WHERE HE BEATS BOTH HIS RIVALS AND THE WET WEATHER. IT TOOK 9 RACES

BREIL
BREIL
46
domino
HONDA

GROUP PHOTOS WITH VALENTINO ROSSI. ABOVE: HELD BY THE MOTO GP WORLD CHAMPIONSHIP PHOTOGRAPHERS. BELOW: SURROUNDED BY HIS TEAM ON THE DAY OF YAMAHA'S TRIUMPH

to wait until 1997 to see the champion, but after Brno success seemed inevitable.

More than just a sports star, Valentino Rossi becomes a media phenomenon and Aprilia, who capitalised on their initial investment (his signing on fee when he won the 125 title had been 190 million old Italian lira – some 100,000 euros) over the three years, now start offering their man serious money. The rider's arrival in the 250 class is sensational: he would have won his debut GP, but for 'team-mate' Tetsuya Harada. The lesson, however, was a good one: the nudge that put Rossi out of the race makes him realise that he is now in with the big boys. He quickly learns the ropes and narrowly misses out on the title in a chaotic race in Buenos Aires, where the World Standings starts out as Capirossi-Harada-Rossi and finishes Capirossi-Rossi-Harada. Valentino then romps to the World Crown during a triumphant 1999 before parting company with Aprilia on the best of terms. There is no lingering bitterness; the two Championship-winning Aprilias with which the company presented him as a parting gift are still proudly displayed in the Rossi household. Honda had simply made him an offer he could not refuse. The biggest motorcycle company in the world were offering him a berth as its official rider, with the team that had belonged to the legendary Mick Doohan. Now things really were getting serious. Rossi is earning huge sums of money and new horizons are opening fast. He moves to London, ostensibly to learn English, but also to escape his fans and anyone who might be interested in his wealth. The champion is an international celebrity, but still has a permanent smile on his lips.

125

NUMBER 1 IS FOR CHAMPIONS, BUT I'LL NEVER ABANDON MY 46

NO.1, BUT IT'S ONLY HIS HAIR. VALENTINO HAS HIS TRADEMARK NUMBER, THE 46 WITH WHICH DAD GRAZIANO WON A RACE

You could be forgiven for imagining that behind Valentino Rossi there is a 'creative team' of set designers, scriptwriters, lyricists, ballad singers and perhaps even a set of doubles holding constant meetings and brainstorming ideas 24 hours a day. The reality, however, is much simpler and, truth be told, much more fun. Anyone who had the privilege of sitting at one of the poolside tables at the Rio de Janeiro Club Nautico during the warm evening of 24 October 1999 and seeing the celebrations for Rossi's second world title would have understood the secret. Two Oba Oba dancers were samba-ing away on the dance floor, when suddenly a group of eye-catching hairy guys in bright costumes burst on to the scene, diverting attention from the local beauties.

The guys were his friends from the Bar dello Sport in

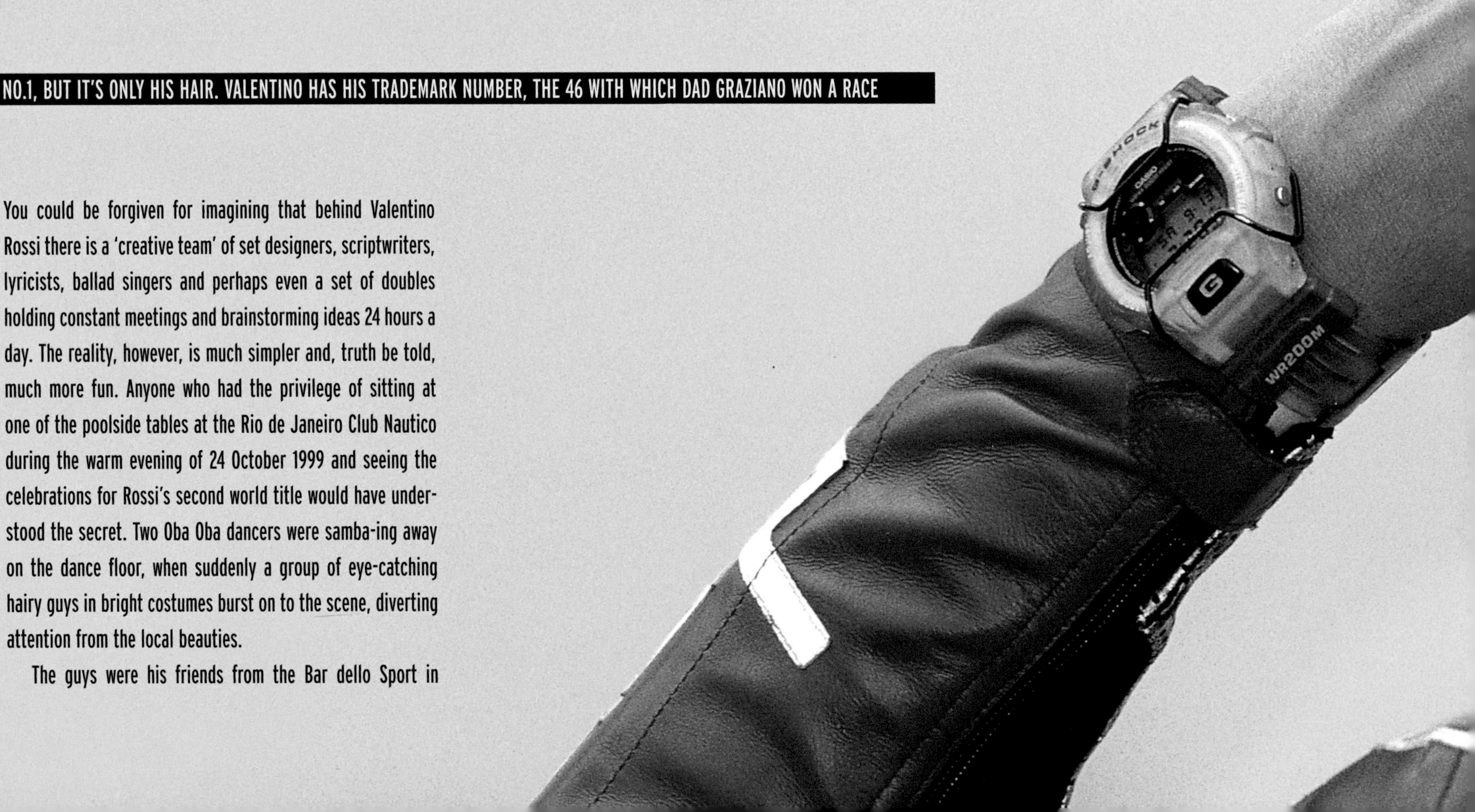

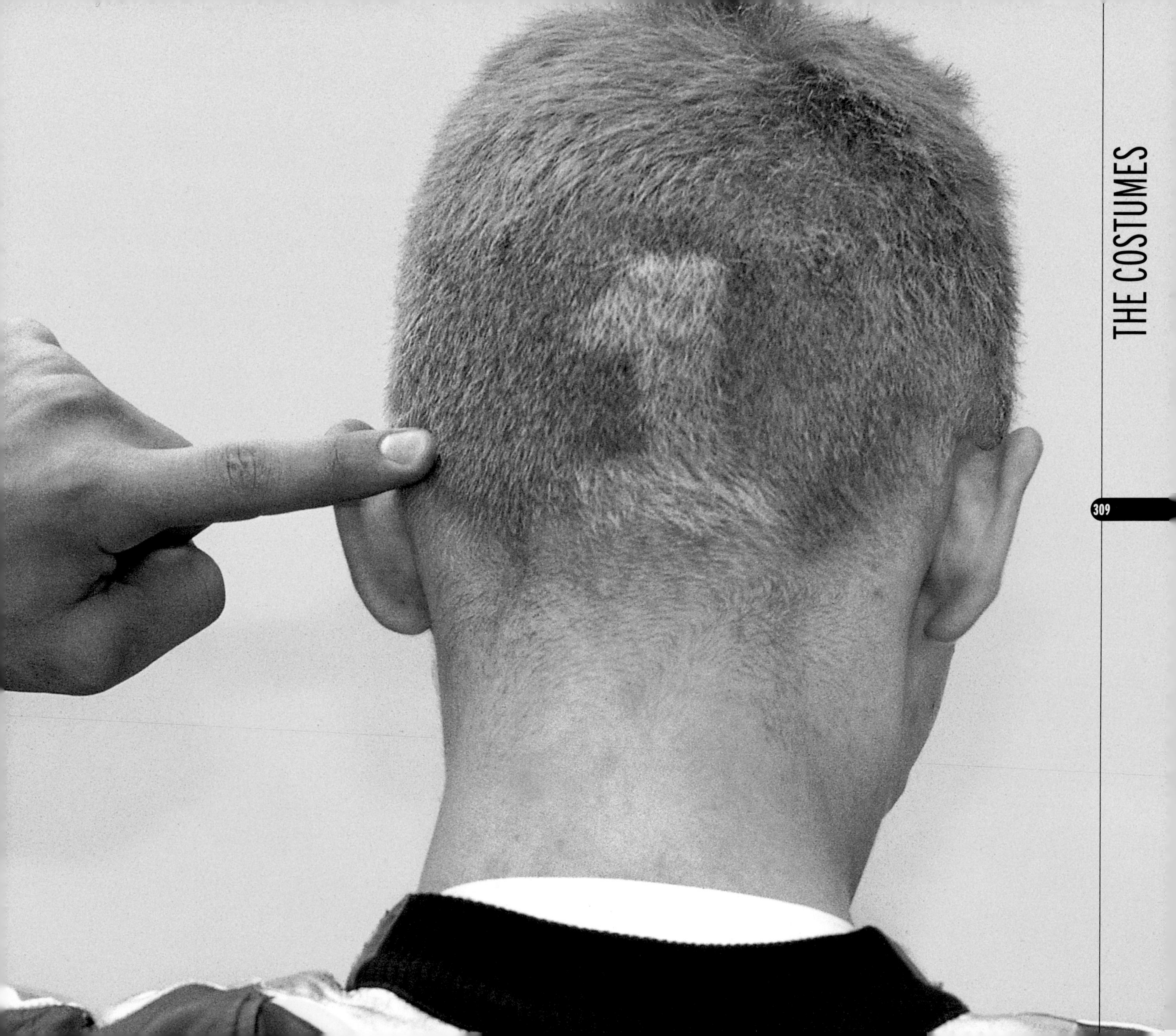

agv
ROSSIFUMI
Comel
polini
agv
domino

STRIKE
LUCKY
Beta

Nastro Azzurro
aprilia
domino
DUNLOP
dainese
ROSSIFUMI
agv
RINGO
agv
domino
Nastro Azzurro
46
dainese
alpinestars

THIS ONE WAS EASY. IT COULD
NLY BE DONE AT DONINGTON

DONINGTON PARK CIRCUIT IS NEAR SHERWOOD FOREST, SO VALENTINO DRESSES UP AS ROBIN HOOD

WHATEVER THE PROPS, IT IS STILL THE ROSSI SHOW. IN GERMANY VALENTINO DRIVES HARD AND R

I LOVE IT EVEN MORE WHEN I'M WINNING . . .

AY WITH IT. HE IS NOT MESSING ABOUT: THE CHAMPIONSHIP IS AT STAKE

 A GIANT NO.1 TO CELEBRATE HIS FIRST WORLD TITLE AT BRNO

NDAGED UP AFTER AN ACCIDENT IN CAPIROSSI'S PORSCHE. VALE NEVER MAKES A SCENE!

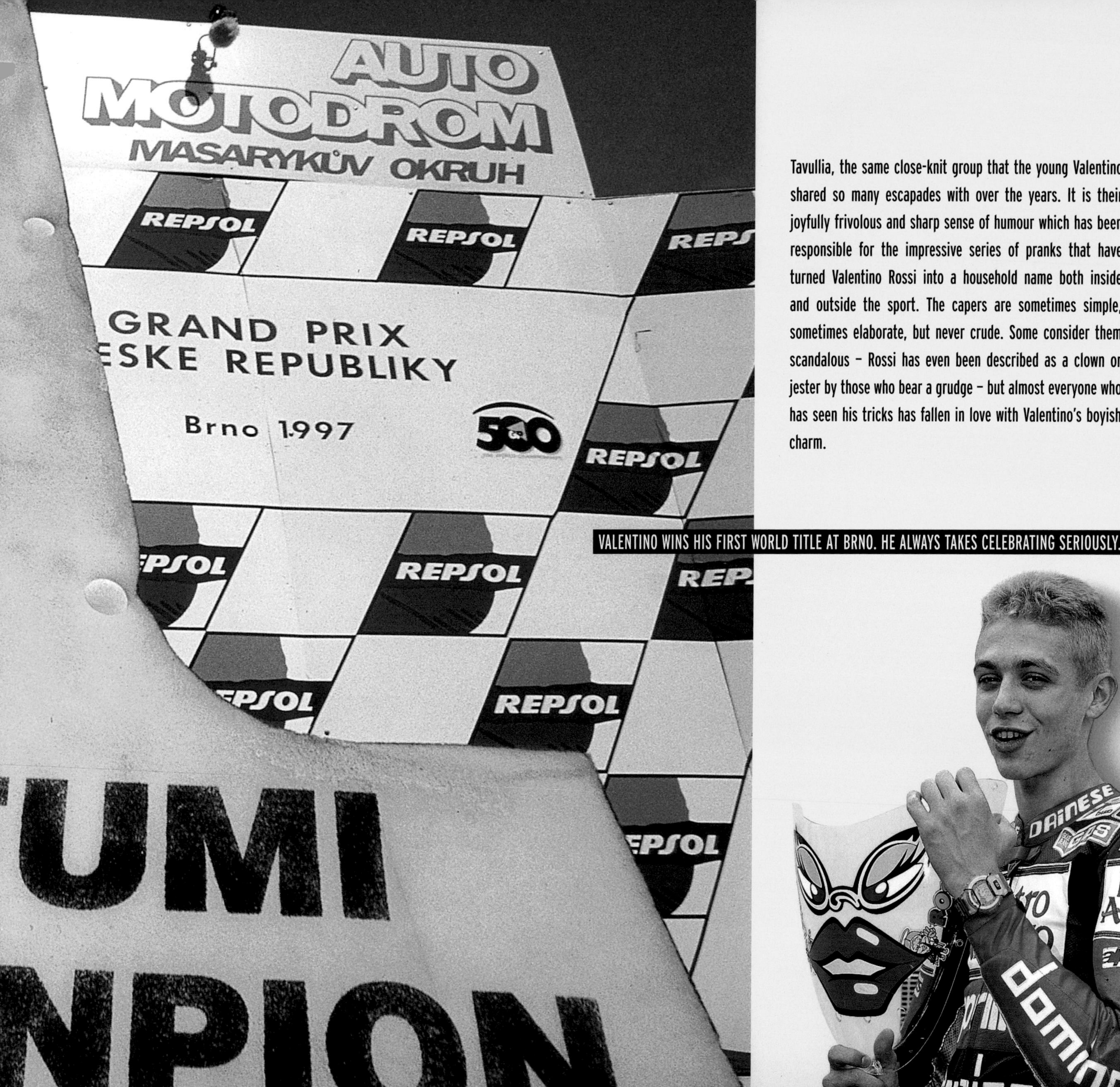

Tavullia, the same close-knit group that the young Valentino shared so many escapades with over the years. It is their joyfully frivolous and sharp sense of humour which has been responsible for the impressive series of pranks that have turned Valentino Rossi into a household name both inside and outside the sport. The capers are sometimes simple, sometimes elaborate, but never crude. Some consider them scandalous – Rossi has even been described as a clown or jester by those who bear a grudge – but almost everyone who has seen his tricks has fallen in love with Valentino's boyish charm.

VALENTINO WINS HIS FIRST WORLD TITLE AT BRNO. HE ALWAYS TAKES CELEBRATING SERIOUSLY.

320 HAT WITH THE WORDS 'NATIONAL EXPORT'. THE GAME WITH HIS FRIENDS BECOMES A CRAZE

I PROMISE. FROM THIS YEAR ON: NO VICTORY, NO GAG

250

IN 250CC, THE PHENOMENAL STREAM OF COSTUMES CONTINUES UNABATED. HIS GAGS, THE POST RACE CABARET, BECOME A SHOW WITHIN A SHOW. THE 'VALENTINOROSSISHOW'

Creating a phenomenon is surprisingly simple. You just have to take your cue from your 'enemy'. The tricky bit is knowing when and how to respond. That was the story during the winter of 1997, when Max Biaggi's affair with Naomi Campbell was splashed all over the tabloids. Max was a three-time champion, Naomi a supermodel. When Biaggi asked for a permanent pass for her as his 'girlfriend', the opportunity was too good to pass up. At Mugello, after the third of what was to become a long series of first-place finishes, a blow-up doll sporting the name 'Claudia Schiffer' rode pillion with Rossi on the victory lap.

It was a typical 'Rossi and Co.' prank that almost everyone enjoyed. It opened up a whole new world and was a new approach to motorcycling entertainment. It was a way of jeering at his rivals, but, paradoxically, could also be used to mock himself.

agv
aprilia
ERICSSON
46
DUNLOP
aprilia

IN TAVULLIA WE HAVE AN 'OLD AGAINST YOUNG' GAME OF FOOTBALL. THEY HAD SOME 'POLLERIA OSVALDO' TOPS MADE AS A JOKE'

LEFT: VALENTINO LOOKS LIKE THE BEACH TYPE. RIGHT: POLLERIA OSVALDO, THE IMAGINARY SPONSC

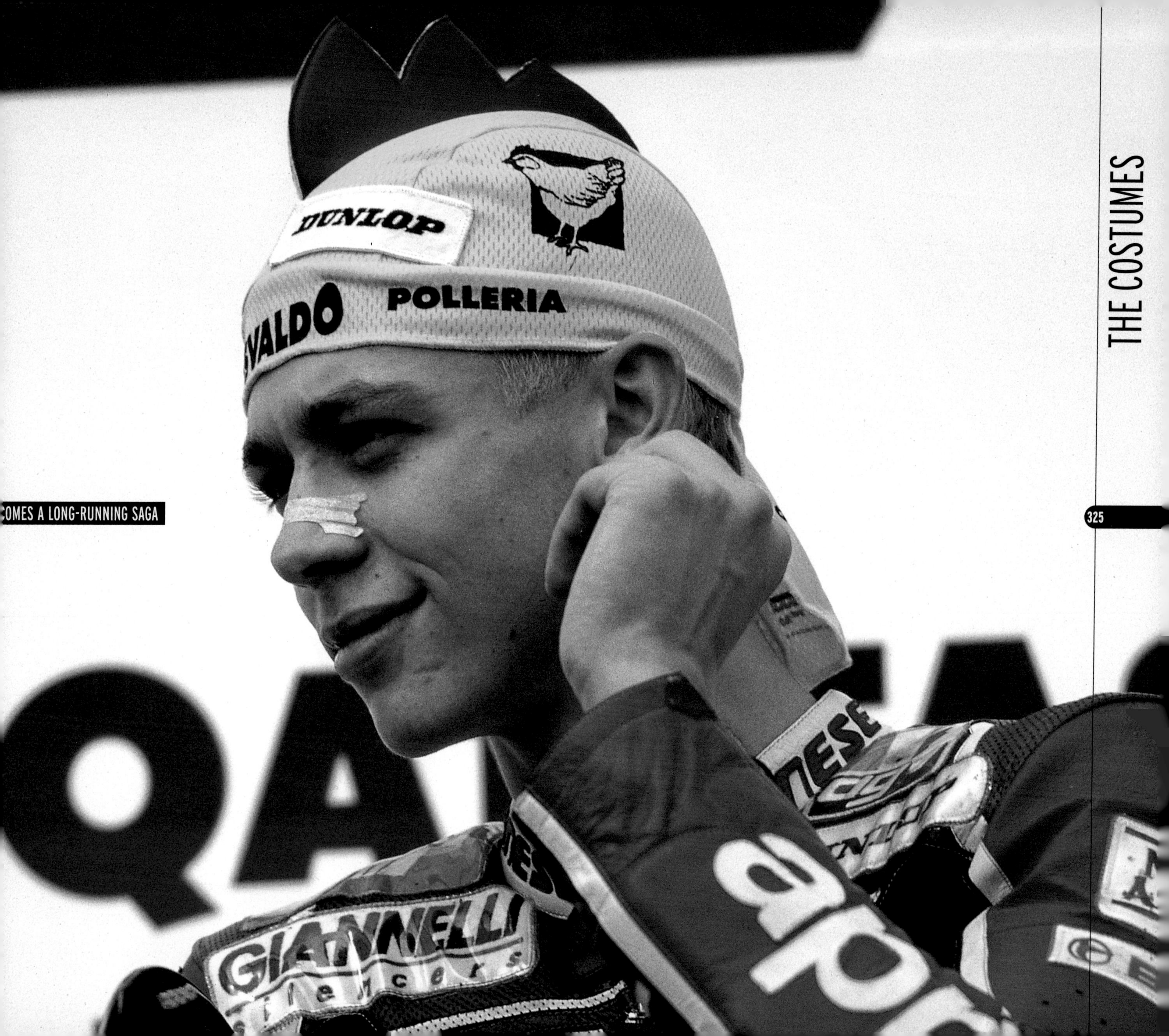
DUNLOP
POLLERIA
VALDO
GIANNELLI

 HIS GUARDIAN ANGEL JOINS THE PARTY IN RIO

VALENTINO ROSSI WINS HIS SECOND WORLD CHAMPIONSHIP AT JACAREPAG

The organisers, recognising that this show-within-a-show could be an easy way to widen their fan base, were encouraging, and so the jokes continued. It was a way of laughing off any mishap. For example, the week before Valentino set off for the Indonesian Grand Prix, he, his friend Capirossi and dad Graziano were in Loris' Porsche after an evening spent partying. The speeding car managed to hit a lamppost before they had even left the car park, with Rossi senior at the wheel. Valentino was in the back seat and bashed his head so hard that he had to go to hospital. The incident, which could have had more serious repercussions, was closed within a few days, when Rossi rode to victory in Indonesia and then appeared on the podium sporting an impressive head bandage.

Some of his celebrations have been spontaneous and ingenious, such as the dash to the toilet after his victory at Jerez in 1999, while others, like the guardian angel who rode pillion on the Aprilia during the Brazilian title celebration of the same year, were sumptuous pantomime. There was also 'il Pollo Osvaldo' (Osvaldo the chicken) of 1998, who emerged from Valentino's imaginary personal sponsor 'Polleria Osvaldo' (Osvaldo's poulterer's) That idea was born after the classic midweek 'old against young' game of football in his home town, which the youngsters lost after playing like 'headless chickens'.

His celebrations are a way of addressing the world on his own terms, in his own paradoxical language. For example, in 2003, four excellent podium finishes had been received almost as defeats. Valentino could not stand that kind of criticism, so instead of sulking and refusing to talk to the press, he set up the convicts' 'slaves to victory' scene; 1-0 Rossi.

 THE SHOW GOES ON IN PREMIER CLASS. FIRST IN 500CC THEN

500 AND MOTOGP

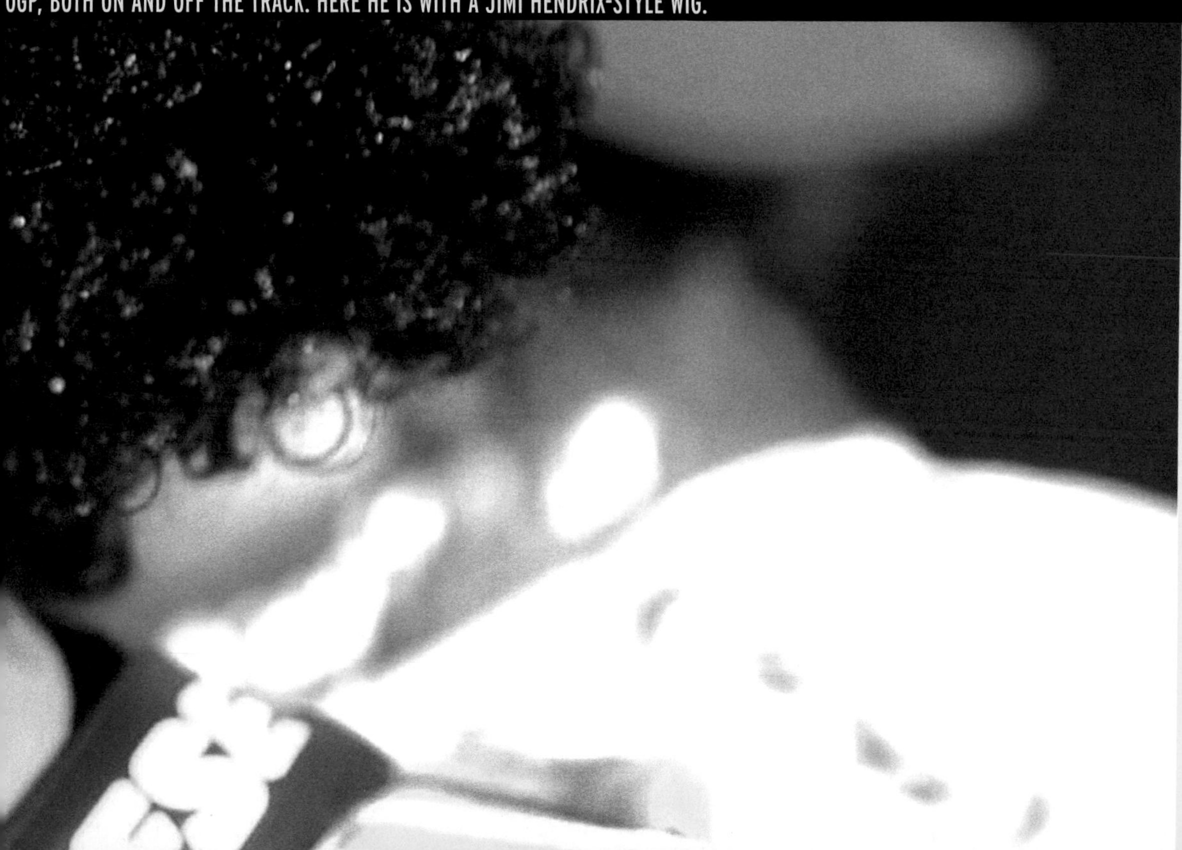

OGP, BOTH ON AND OFF THE TRACK. HERE HE IS WITH A JIMI HENDRIX-STYLE WIG.

There was more irreverence after he won the Malaysian Grand Prix. Rossi's response to being penalised in Qatar, when his mechanics cleaned part of the track in violation of the rules, was to scrub the Sepang asphalt in full view of the world, wearing a top emblazoned with the (imaginary) 'La Rapida' cleaning company logo.

But sometimes there were mistakes, too. His biggest error came at Mugello in 1998, when a fantastic beach scene had been prepared for the lap of honour. The race itself was won by his team-mate, the 'old man', Marcellino Lucchi, but Rossi could not resist showing the world what he and his friends had prepared. He appeared on the podium in shorts and flip-flops, overshadowing his friend and team-mate's delight at having

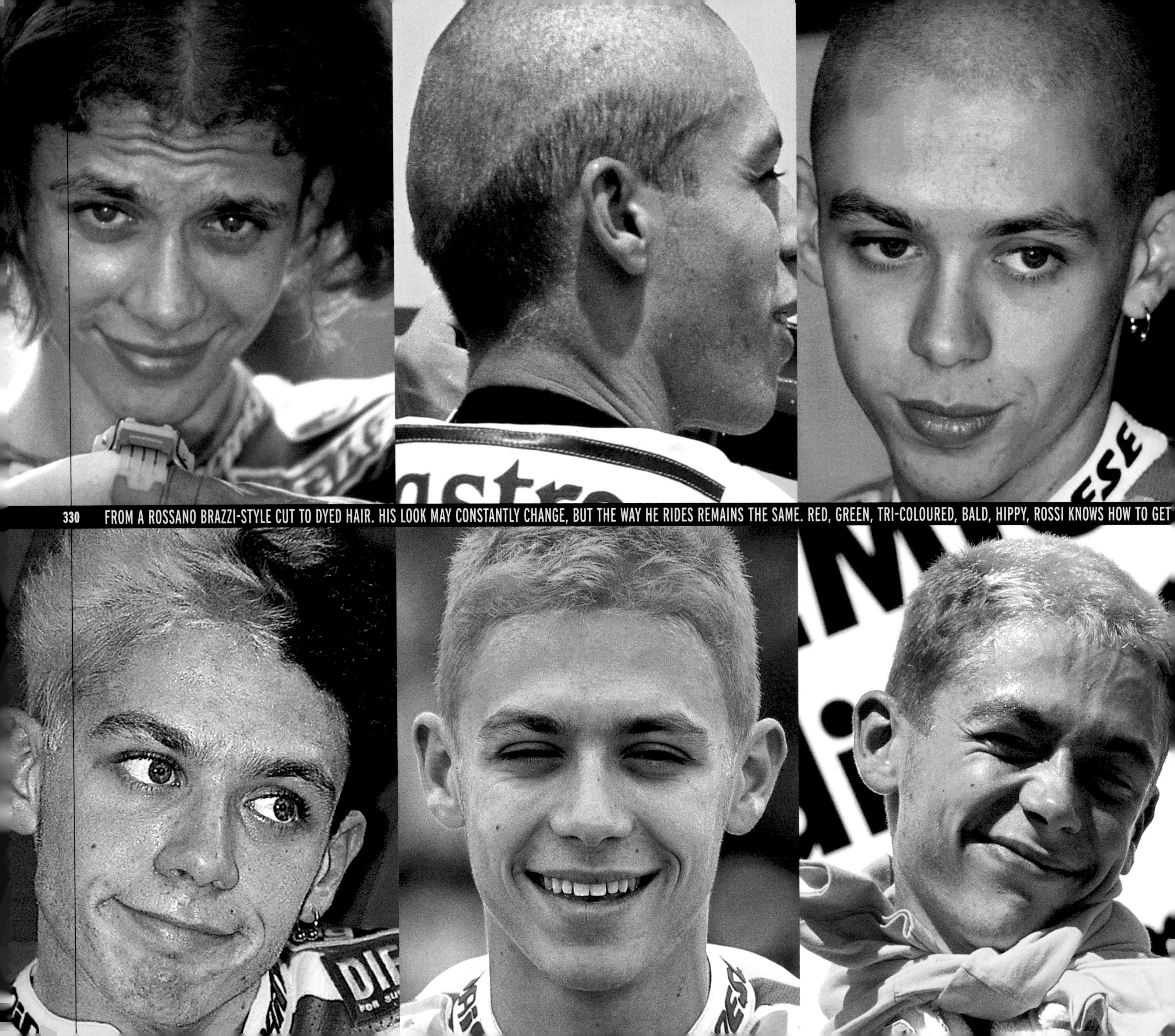

FROM A ROSSANO BRAZZI-STYLE CUT TO DYED HAIR. HIS LOOK MAY CONSTANTLY CHANGE, BUT THE WAY HE RIDES REMAINS THE SAME. RED, GREEN, TRI-COLOURED, BALD, HIPPY, ROSSI KNOWS HOW TO GET

RIVALS. THE SUNGLASSES CHANGE TOO – BUT THAT MIGHT HAVE SOMETHING TO DO WITH HIS SPONSORS . . .

CONDEMNED TO WIN. A SLAVE TO VICTORY AFTER FOUR RACES WITHOUT SUCCESS. AT BRNO, THE CHAINS COME OFF AND HE RIDES TO THE 2003 TITLE

WE COME UP WITH
THE COSTUMES IN THE BAR

SPEED TRAP AT MUGELLO: VALENTINO GOES TOO FAST AND IS FINED

OFFICIAL FAN CLUB
46
VALENTINO ROSSI
TAVULLIA

TOGP TITLE NO.1 IS CELEBRATED IN BRAZIL. A 7 FOR SHEENE IN AUSTRALIA

KERAKOLL
TRIBÙ DEI
CAMEL
M1
YAMAHA

DOCTOR ROSSI SAYS THE YAMAHA IS OKAY . . .

'I PROMISED I'D TAKE HIM UP ON THE PODIUM'. SOME CHAMPAGNE FOR CIRO

agv
KERAKOLL
CHE
SPETTACOLO
46
GAULOISES

agv
ROGER
ENERGIE
BREIL WATCHES
MANPOWER
domino
HONDA
Verlicchi

THE CLEANING COMPANY. VALENTINO ROSSI AND HIS FRIENDS RESPOND TO THE PENALTY IN QATAR. VALE DOMINATES THE 2004 SEPANG GP THEN, AFTER THE RACE, CLEANS UP THE CHAMPIONSHIP

won his first Grand Prix at the age of 41. 'From now on, the show goes hand-in-hand with victory.' he promised, and stuck to his word.

There were, of course, several other gags that unfortunately never saw the light of day. There was the surfing scene at Mugello in 2001, to 'celebrate' a fall in the rain, and the 6-metre-high bell that was taken to Germany to celebrate a first outing for Don Cesare, the Tavullia parish priest for whom Rossi had been altar boy. That one was shelved thanks to a Sete Gibernau attack on the last corner. We also missed out on the gigantic sign intended to ridicule the fine received for the dash to the toilet at Jerez in '99. The rain in France put paid to that one, with the race's subsequent restart washing away the chance of either victory or jest.

Fortunately we were not deprived of what could, thanks to its simplicity and effect, be the perfect representation of the relationship between Valentino and his childhood group of friends. It was on 2 June 2002 and the blue, white and orange Honda had just streaked past the chequered flag at Mugello. Suddenly two grave-looking 'officials', red stop sign in hand, appeared at the end of the straight and proceeded to book the young rider for speeding and disturbing the World Championship's peace. Fantastic!

ALWAYS SPECIAL EVEN WHEN HE COMES OFF

VALENTINO ROSSI FINISHED A 'RESPECTABLE' 7TH IN THE 'FALLERS LIST' IN '96, WITH 10 TUMBLES: BUT THE FALLS BECOME RARER AS HIS CAREER PROGRESSES

Valentino Rossi did not see his first Grand Prix with his father Graziano. It would have been the logical way to begin, rider to rider, but things did not turn out that way. Instead, his first GP experience was during the summer of 1994, when the young Rossi went to see Dr Claudio Costa, the specialist motorcycle racers' doctor, in the Brno paddock. The young man was looking for some treatment for a bad foot caused by a scooter accident, to enable him to race in the finals of the Italian Sport Production Championship. The trip, undertaken with his faithful friend Uccio and Uccio's dad Rino Salucci, who was later President of the Tavullia fan club, must have been a success, since the young Vale won the title – although not without controversy, as we have seen.

Rossi and his friends lived fast and furious lives, with the

A 'PHENOMENAL' CAREER IS JUST BEGINNING: THE ERRORS OF YOUTH ARE INEVITABLE

MY LEFT FOOT HAS BEEN TENDER SINCE 1994,
WHEN I WAS HIT BY A CAR WHILE ON A FRIEND'S SCOOTER

JAPANESE GP 1997

 A SLIP WITH THE APRILIA AT SUZUKA. WHEN YOU'RE 18

THE DESIRE F

TORY CAN PROVE COSTLY. BUT AGGRESSIVE RIDING PAYS OFF IN THE END, TAKING THE YOUNG ROSSI TO HIS FIRST WORLD CHAMPIONSHIP WITH 11 WINS

MUGELLO 1999: 'THE PEOPLE ARE CRAZY, THEY INVADED THE TRACK.

I WAS SWAMPED BEFORE I COULD REACH MY FAN CLUB, AND FELL OFF’

 RODEO IN VALENCIA: IN 2000, ON THE HONDA, FIRST HE RECOVERS, THEN COMES OFF A FEW LAPS LATER. TOKYO, 2003, ON THE RC211V, VALE RIDES LIKE A COWBOY, ACROBAT STYLE

I EXPECTED TO FALL, BUT THE BIKE RECOVERED SWEETLY AND I STAYED ON

VALENCIA GP 2000

REPSOL
GAS
SHOWA
NGK
HONDA

I FELL AT BARCELONA AND DONINGTON AND WENT ON TO WIN

AUSTRALIAN GP 2001

IN AUSTRALIA HE FALLS IN PRACTICE THEN WINS BY A WHISKER

ROSSI ON THE TARMAC AT PHILLIP ISLAND. BUT IT'S ONLY FRIDAY AND THERE'S PLENTY OF TIME TO RECOVER.

HE GOES ON TO BEAT MAX AND LORIS BY MILLISECONDS

I HIT A CRACK AND LOST CONTROL

AUSTRALIAN GP 2001

'I ALMOST MANAGED TO RECOVER BUT THEN I LOST THE BIKE. I'M CALM: IT DIDN'T CROSS MY MIND THAT THINGS MIGHT GO BADLY WRONG'

46
Nastro Azzurro
ENERGIE
THE DOCTOR
MANPOWER
domino
HONDA
HONDA
PlayStation.2
NSR
VALE 46
polini
Birra · Beer
Nastro Azzurro
HRC
Verlicchi
polini
Birra · Beer
Nastro Azzurro
MICHELIN
brembo
SHOWA
NGK
RK
TAKASAGO CHAIN
AFAM
BIOFOX
REPSOL YPF
Beta
MICHELIN

SEPANG 2000: WHAT A LANDING

young rider discovering the bitter taste of tarmac very early on. He was constantly on the move on his scooter or in the Ape van, driving around the hills of Pesaro with his pals. Their favourite testing ground was the Rossifumi Bend, which curves up at the end of the village, where the monument to the fallen soldiers stands. For a while it was even known as the Caroni Bend, in honour of one of the gang who had crashed his scooter on a number of occasions. There were also close encounters with the local police, who ironically built the new police station a stone's throw from the champion's house. The occasional tumble was always inevitable.

Even on the day Rossi officially began his career as a World Championship rider there was talk of cuts and scrapes. Team Sacchi presented their team for the new season, including the great Italian prodigy, on a cold morning in early February 1996. No one could fail to notice the plaster over Rossi's right eyebrow. What had happened? 'My Mum was making salad, and she slammed the door on my eye when she was getting the oil,' he explained with a captivating smile. It was only long afterwards that the truth emerged: it was due to yet another road accident, this time with the Piaggio Ape.

He enjoyed taking risks, of course, and also indulged in the classic teenage penchant for breaking the rules. Things changed, however, when Vale started taking his racing seriously. However, the rider still made a 'flying' start to his World Championship career with 10 falls in his first season, a tally which put him in an 'impressive' seventh place in the standings for Championship falls. Among them was the unenviable record of four tumbles in a row, all in the Brazilian GP which, unfortunately for the man from Tavullia, was extended by an extra day for additional practice.

HONDA
46
BREIL

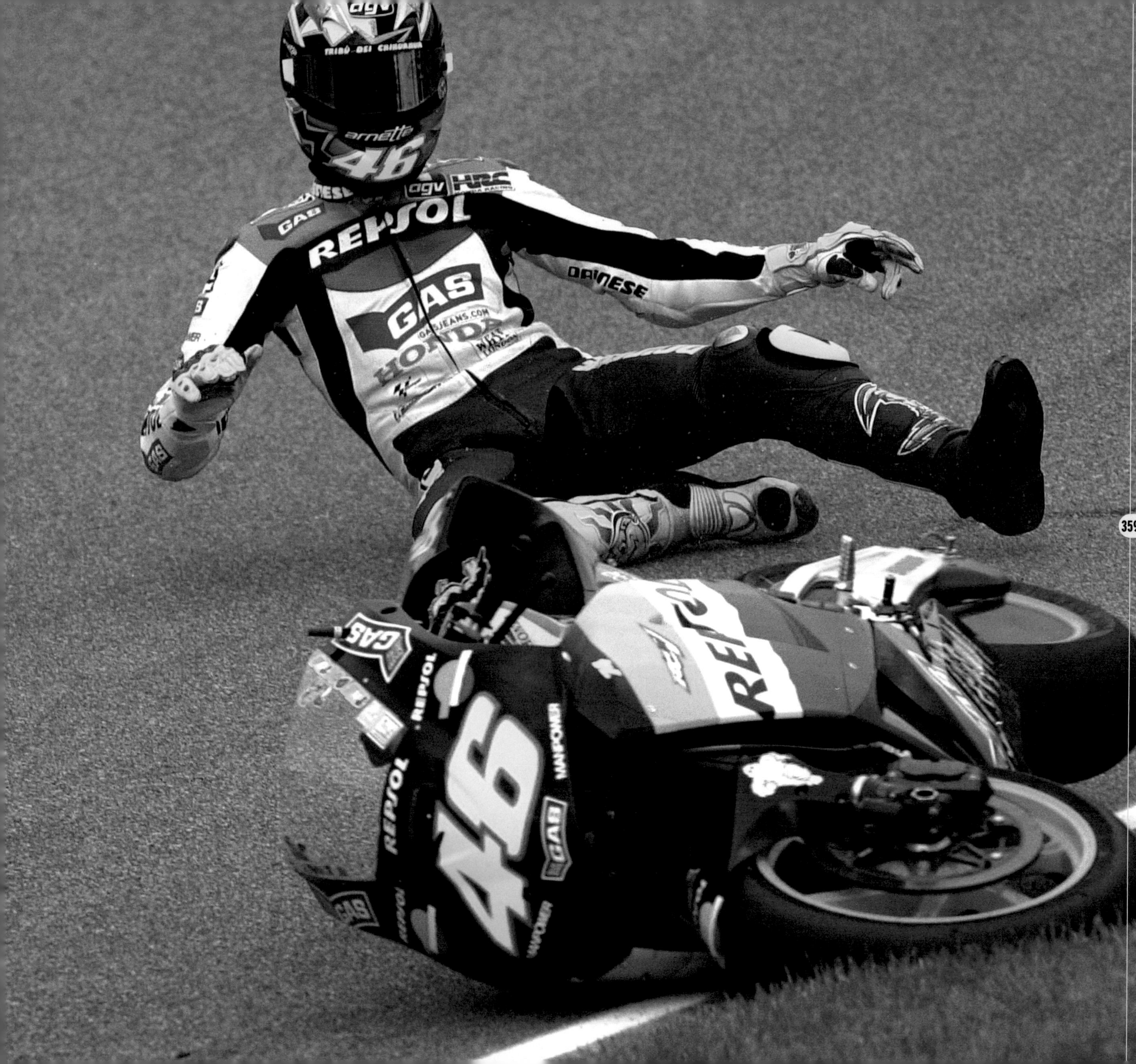
agv
46
REPSOL
GAS
HONDA
DAINESE
REPSOL
46
REPSOL
GAS

A RARE SIGHT IN 2003: ROSSI ON THE GROUND WITH HIS HONDA SLIDING AWAY.

NOTHING SERIOUS: I DIDN'T NOTICE A BIT OF WATER AND FOUND MYSELF ON THE GROUND

GERMAN GP 2003

ERROR IN PRACTICE, CAUSED BY A PUDDLE. HE WOULD GO ON TO WIN THE MOTOGP TITLE FROM GIBERNAU BY 80 POINTS

ALL IT TOOK WAS A PUDDLE;
THAT'S WHY I HATE RACING IN THE WET

GERMAN GP 2003

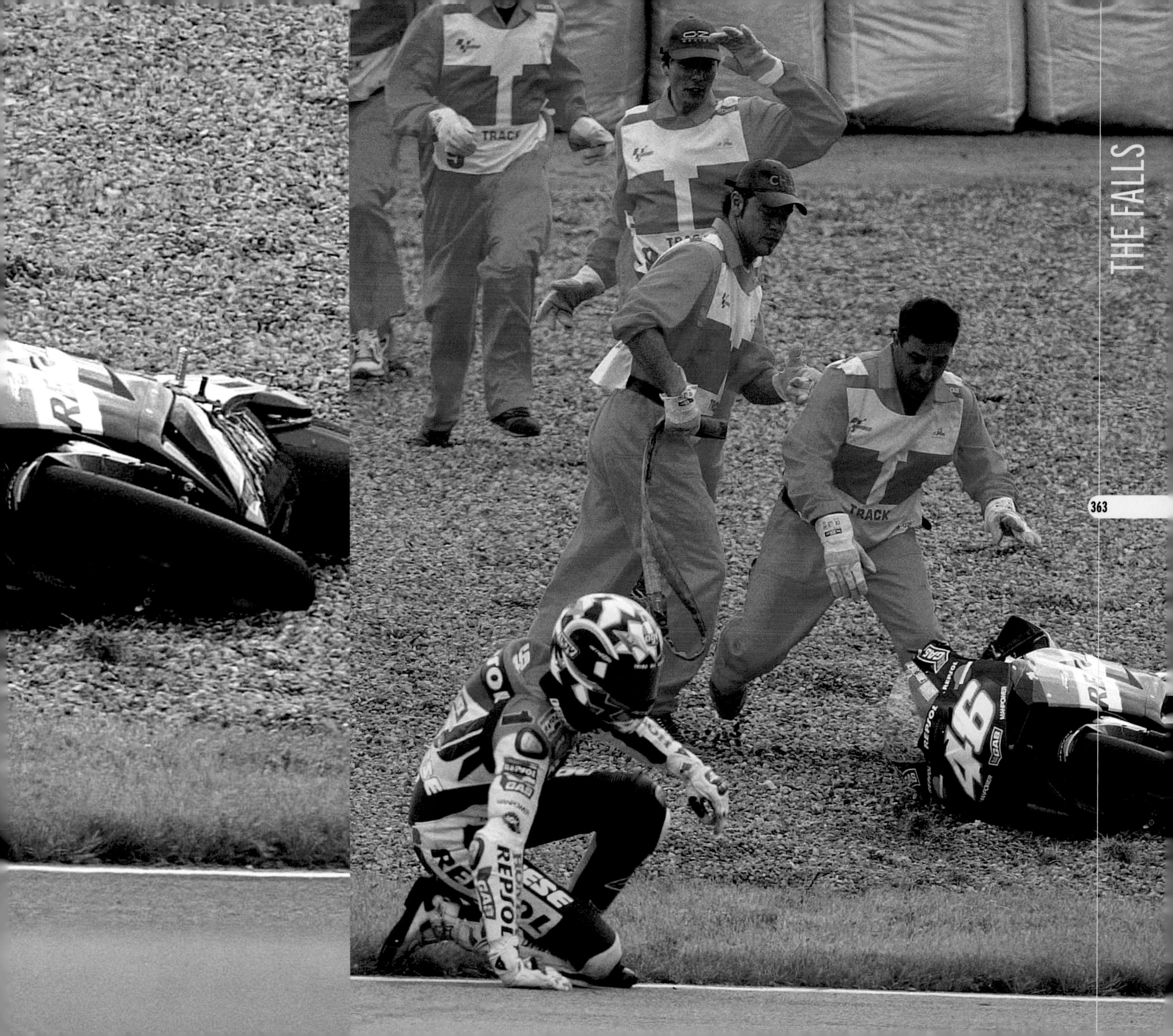
TRACK
TRACK
REPSOL
REPSOL
46

REPSOL
HONDA
REPSOL
GAS
HONDA

DAINESE
HONDA
GAS

FLOORED AT A MERE 60KPH. BUT THE 2002 TUMBLE DURING PRACTICE SESSIONS FOR THE BRITISH GRAND PRIX AT DONINGTON WILL BE REMEMBERED AS

OF HIS MOST SPECTACULAR. VALE'S HONDA SEEMED BEWITCHED AND FLUNG HIM INTO THE AIR. A FRIGHTENING FALL, LUCKILY WITHOUT SERIOUS CONSEQUENCES

'IT'S ALL A BLUR. I SAW UKAWA GO DOWN, THEN I FELL. I'VE GOT A BAD HEADACHE'

From 1997, however, things changed. There were still tumbles, but almost always of the 'functional' kind. You can fall because you do not know your limit – the meaningless kind, or you can come off when you are trying to understand your limit. And the Rossi who emerged in 1997 (4 falls in 15 races), the one who never stopped winning in all categories, seemed to have chosen the latter path. The champion developed a keen 'seventh sense', which enabled him to minimise the risks. A slide at the last corner of the Johor GP in Indonesia at the beginning of '98, when his line 'came into contact' with that of 'team-mate' Tetsuya Harada, was an eye-opener for Rossi. First it showed him that 250cc was more demanding than 125, but secondly, and more importantly, that Japanese riders were not all as friendly as the ones he had always adored.

Valentino had another mid-air experience in his beloved Australia, at Phillip Island, when he was taking stock of the 500 in the winter of 2000. 'I've never been that high,' he said afterwards. 2004 was a year of lessons. His new Yamaha put him to the test on more than one occasion. At the Jerez GP it rained on his parade after being sunny throughout the practice sessions, and an incredibly spectacular close shave convinced the Italian that it was not to be his day. In Brazil, a few weeks later, he wanted to see just what his new bike was capable of. During that particular race, the Yamaha was not in the best of shape and Sete Gibernau, the champion's most dangerous rival, had already fallen – all good reasons for playing it safe. However, for Rossi the only way of finding the thin line between winning and taking things too far is by constantly pushing the boundaries.

THE MARSHALS ARRIVE IMMEDIATELY AND ROSSI, STILL IN SHOCK, RECEIVES FIRST AID, INITIALLY IN THE TRACKSIDE MOBILE CLINIC, THEN IN NOTTINGHA

SPITAL. IS THE CHAMP KO? NO, HE'S OK AND RECOVERS TO WIN THE RACE

GAULOISES
YAMAHA
GAULOISES
YAMAHA
GAULOISES
GAULOISES
M1
ÖHLINS
MAGNETI MARELLI
YAMAHA
MOTUL
MICHELIN
NGK
SPARK PLUGS
2D

IT WAS TERRIFYING.
EVERY TIME I BRAKED
I ALMOST CAME OFF

SPANISH GP 2004

46

IO, ROSSI GOES DOWN A FEW LAPS AFTER GIBERNAU. THE CHAMPIONSHIP WAS WIDE OPEN AGAIN

It was in Rio that Valentino found out the hard way exactly where the Yamaha's limits lay.

The 'secret' Ferrari F1 tests were also a driving lesson of sorts. You would have expected caution to be the order of the day when sitting in the driving seat of such a valuable and expensive machine. The official line had labelled it 'a reward for his achievements', but for Rossi it was an opportunity to see just how far he could push himself on four wheels. The test comprised one screeching stop with smoking brakes, an exit via the escape lane and a sortie on to the grass – Formula One motocross style. But none of his driving excesses were gratuitous; the purpose was always to further his understanding.

Rossi's worst fall comes on a Friday morning in July 2002, during the free practice sessions at Donington, a track which is slippery at the best of times. He is on Goddards hairpin, just before the home straight, doing a mere 60kph or so, but in a spot where eight other riders have already hit the deck. It should not have been nearly as dangerous as the super-fast Cramer, for example, where the hugely powerful MotoGP bikes went at some 200kph and where his team-mate Tohru Ukawa had completely wiped out a couple of minutes earlier. The practice sessions are nearing their close when Valentino, without really knowing how, is sent flying. It is a spectacular, maybe even artistic, fall and leaves him with a small fracture and, more seriously, a blow to the head. The Italian has to go to hospital, but tests show that he got off relatively lightly and needs no more than an afternoon's rest. On the Saturday he feels fine and is back in the saddle, coming fifth in the free practice session and producing a record-breaking time in the official qualifiers. 'It was no miracle, just a pole position,' he says afterwards, which was true, because the real surprise was reserved for Sunday: another victory, of course.

ON THE GRAVEL DURING THE WARM-UP FOR THE FRENCH GP

A BLEEDING LITTLE FINGER AFTER COMING OFF DURING THE CONTROVERSIAL QATAR GRAND PRIX

CRAZY ABOUT RALLYING AND **FERRARI RED**

RALLYING IS VALENTINO'S GREATEST PASSION: HE LOVES 'DRIVING SIDEWAYS' WITH CARS TOO. UNLIKE ON A BIKE, HE'S NOT UNBEATABLE ON

Valentino Rossi is not your typical-looking athlete. Under the leathers beats the heart of a great competitor, but he is not exactly a muscle man. That said, it is wiser not to mention this in his presence, as he can be a touch sensitive on the subject. 'You've got to stop saying that I don't train. I go to the gym all the time,' he says peevishly when the subject of how physically tough it must be to ride MotoGP comes up. There are certainly no doubts over his riding ability, despite the lack of brawn. But it is hardly surprising that he finds training a chore; how can a bench press and weights machine, or worse still, swimming-pool lane be expected to stimulate the competitive juices of a motorcycling champion?

Valentino did undertake some physical conditioning when he moved from 125cc to the quarter-litre class in 1998, and more when he graduated to the 500cc two years later. In both

FOUR WHEELS OFFROAD, BUT WHO CARES. IT'S FUN!

 IN ACTION WITH THE PEUGEOT 206 WRC IN THE 2002 BRITISH RALLY, THE LAST ROUND OF THE WORLD RALLY CHAMPIONSHIP. ROSSI AND CARLO CASSINA, HIS CO-DRIVER, DO NOT LAST LONG. 20KM INTO T

ST SPECIAL STAGE THE CAR ENDS UP IN A DITCH: EFFORTS TO EXTRACT IT PROVE FRUITLESS

cases it took him only a few laps to realise that racing more powerful bikes requires more strength, and as a consequence a personal trainer was hired. Vale undertook the training programmes, but only for as long as it took him to gain the strength necessary to race.

In the millions of photos that have been taken of Valentino Rossi, it is extremely difficult – perhaps even impossible – to find a picture of him out jogging or using a piece of gym equipment. These are activities in which effort is the end in itself, with no further satisfaction.

For other pastimes, we are spoilt for choice. Take the example of football. As everyone knows, it is Italy's national sport and Rossi is, of course, crazy about it. On the pitch he is a decent left-footed midfielder with a penchant for getting forward. Valentino occasionally turns out for the relatively unknown national motorbike riders' side and more often in the regular Fan Club v. Dora (the organisers of the motorcycling World Championship) games. Unlike others, he has not managed, or has not wanted, to fulfil the dream of playing alongside any of his favourite players, not even Ronaldo. He does, however, have the great Brazilian's shirt in his souvenir cabinet, and regards it as one of his most treasured possessions. Valentino is not a huge fan of swimming, or the sea, in spite of his house in Ibiza. Snow is much more his thing. In fact, his first public appearances were during the riders' skiing weeks that took place at Livigno. The winter of 1990 was made particularly memorable by an irritating 11-year-old kid with an angelic face, who followed Loris Capirossi around all day, constantly asking him questions.

Vale's passion for snow has stayed with him, but he has moved with the times and now prefers snowboarding to skiing,

Marlboro
vodafone
OLYMPUS
FIAT

PRIL 2004. VALE TEST-DRIVES THE FERRARI F2004 AT FIORANO. 50 LAPS IN TOTAL, NOT ALL SUCCESSFUL. HIS FASTEST TIME IS 59.1 SECS, ONLY 3.5 SECONDS SLOWER THAN SCHUMI'S RECORD

which he assures us that he is pretty good at. His passion for the slopes has remained undimmed, in spite of the incident in January 2005 when he crashed into a skier who went as far as reporting the star to the police.

These are pleasures, but what really rocks Vale's boat is anything with an engine, whether on two or four wheels. For him driving always turns into a challenge, and has been a passion since before he could walk. A lot of this must have come from dad Graziano's passion for racing motorbikes – the youngster's first means of transport was a child's motorcycle. He very quickly moved on to Go-Karts and was a promising racer, winning the regional championship, but was forced on to two wheels because of the cost. Then came motorbikes, both on and off-road. But Valentino has never been a fan of traditional motocross – 'I don't like flying, I like to keep my feet on the ground, so jumping with a motorcycle isn't for me' – or conventional Supermotard. Instead of these, what the teenager really enjoyed was 'quarry riding', a style he and Rossi senior developed together.

Perhaps this could help to explain his driving skills on the track. It was nothing new, of course, the great Americans of the '70s and '80s graduated from very similar dirt tracks. It was on dirt that the champion-to-be refined his ability to control a sliding motorcycle, a skill that was later to prove so useful when riding 500cc MotoGP bikes to the limit. For a long time, the quarry was a constant feature of Saturday afternoons. Behind closed doors, on different bikes to the ones he used professionally, this was the setting for some crazy races.

He never stops racing, whether it is with his closest friends (all excellent bikers too), Graziano, or with various other riders who have the honour of moving in the 'right circles'.

I'M AN INTER FAN BECAUSE OF RONALDO. WHEN WE BEAT MILAN OR JUVE I SPEND AGES ON THE PHONE TO MY FRIENDS, GLOATING

 SUPERMOTARD, GO-KARTING, SNOW MOBILE, FOOTBALL AND TENNIS. VALE IS AN ALL-ROUND SPORTSMAN. 'AS A KID I PLAYED FOOTBALL, LIKE ALL ITALIANS. I LOVE IT, IT'S RELAXING AND FUN'

ROSSI USES HIS LEFT, BOTH ON THE PITCH AND ON COURT

'BETWEEN 14 AND 17 I WAS MAD ABOUT SCOOTERS. WE USED TO HAVE RACES TO SEE WHOSE WAS FASTEST.

RFING? I JUST HAD SOME FAKE PHOTOS TAKEN AT PHILLIP ISLAND.' AT SEA HE USES A SPEEDBOAT AND EVEN HAS A BOAT LICENCE

'I OFTEN USE A BIKE ON THE ROAD TOO. IT'S A BIT DANGEROUS BUT YOU FEEL FREE AND DON'T HAVE TO QUEUE'

Vale's love for rallying was also born on that short, but challenging, dirt track. He has always followed the sport with the commitment worthy of a professional. He described his first car, a Subaru Impreza, as 'a car that a housewife can take to the supermarket, but in which you can do some amazing things'. Valentino took part in the Monza Rally in 1997, where he showed the world that he was a driver quick to learn new skills, in spite of the fact that there has been no shortage of incidents en route. The worst of these came in 2002, during the legendary RAC British Rally, for which he had prepared extremely carefully and had an all-but-official Peugeot 206 and a following worthy of an absolute star. He was unfortunately forced to retire after just a few kilometres: 'I was unlucky when my tyres went a few centimetres too far over the edge of a small ditch. There were loads of spectators a few hundred metres further on who would have been able to help me get the car out.' It was then that the motorcyclist realised that rallying is a bit too demanding for someone with his lifestyle, who spends such a lot of his time sleeping. He had already once missed the start of a rally, at Monza in 2000, when he slept through his alarm and arrived to find the race underway, much to the chagrin of his father. So he changed tack, deciding 'it would perhaps be easier, being a motorcycle racer, to get my head around racing on the track. At least the setting would be familiar.' Having made the decision, he went straight to the top and spent a day with Ferrari, at whom he had previously more or less turned up his nose. It was the fulfilment of every motor sport fan's wildest dreams; a day's testing which he passed with flying colours. Was it merely a day out, or would it lead to something more . . . ?

THE **SHOW** MUST GO ON

WE'RE BOTH LEGENDS,
I WANT TO MEET HIM

MICHAEL JORDAN (VALENCIA 2004)

VALENTINO WITH BASKETBALL LEGEND MICHAEL JORDAN. JORDAN IS A HUGE MOTORBIKE FAN. HE HAS A SUPERSPORT TEAM IN THE US AND DROVE THE DUCATI BIPOSTO AT VALENCIA

In the Salone delle Feste at the Quirinale Palace, then Italian President Carlo Azeglio Ciampi approaches with a smile on his lips, for the formal welcome. 'Valentino, congratulations. We enjoy your victories very much.' 'Thank you, Mr President; I'm a fan of yours too.' That is more or less how the conversation would have gone had it taken place, but unfortunately, on that day in early June 2003 when the President was meeting the motorcycling champions, Valentino found he had a prior commitment. Had he been there, however, the conversation would certainly have flowed easily. Valentino has an extraordinary ability to be, and make people feel, at ease, whether he is talking to a mechanic or the President.

It is a natural gift. The image of Valentino Rossi has not

Nastro
Azzurro

 ROSSI: CHAMPION AMONG CHAMPIONS. WITH PHIL READ (ABOVE), JACQUES VILLENEUVE (BELOW) AND JUAN PABLO MONTOYA (CENTRE)

IN THE MOBILE CLINIC WITH DR COSTA AND ALEX ZANARDI. BELOW, WITH JEAN ALESI

ROSSI READS THE SPORTS NEWS, MOTORSPORT FIRST,

JOURNALISTS?
SOME ARE BRILLIANT, SOME ARE RUBBISH.
I'LL GIVE THEM 5 OUT OF 10 ON AVERAGE

OURSE, THEN THE FOOTBALL, ESPECIALLY ANYTHING ON INTER MILAN

been carefully constructed through any concerted media strategy; it is a way of presenting himself which has come naturally to Rossi from years of being at the centre of attention. At barely 18, fresh from his victory in the 125 Championship, the teenager was welcomed to *La Gazzetta dello Sport* by the editor, Candido Cannavò, who immediately became 'overwhelmingly candid' as Rossi put it. This was long before Italian comedian Maurizio Crozza had come up with his celebrated Cannavò impression, which just goes to show that Valentino is quick, nimble and straight to the point both on a motorbike and in public. No question embarrasses Rossi. He used to just come out with the first thing that came into his head. Now, older and wiser, he thinks for a moment before answering, trying to anticipate any potential problems he is unwilling to face. And then out comes his response, pertinent and never boring.

Then there is his innocent, cherubic face. But there is a sting in the tail, always ready to strike the latest victim without seemingly offending anyone, another reason why the media love him.

After Rossi's first title with Aprilia, he was invited to Mediaset to record an interview for Italian television. Suddenly, out of the blue, came the question: 'Would you like to present *Studio Sport* instead of Guido Meda?' The response was instantaneous and the fledgling presenter was a revelation in his 'new role'. Mr Meda only kept his job because you earn more from racing than presenting . . .

The secret with Valentino is simple: attract his attention and get him involved.

Rossi carries out his duties diligently, but becomes

 ROSSI ALSO STARS IN ADVERTS: ONE WAS SUCH A HIT THAT HIS SPONSOR GAVE HIM A PERSONALISED CINQUECENTO. YELLOW OF COURSE

Guardami negli occhi e ripeti.
se bevo non guido, se bevo non guido, se bevo non guido.
D'ora in poi non potrai fare a meno di pensare a Valentino e a questo annuncio.
E ti ricorderai che c'è più gusto a bere senza guidare e a guidare senza avere bevuto.
Ti ricorderai che c'è più gusto per la vita.
C'è più gusto a essere italiani.
Nastro Azzurro
EXPORT QUALITY
Motomondiale 1999
Nastro Azzurro e Valentino Rossi
Campioni del Mondo classe 250
Valentino campione del mondo! Mancava solo il titolo, alle più entusiasmanti pagine del motociclismo moderno scritte sulle piste di tutto il mondo. È l'autore di questo capolavoro il titolo l'ha vinto, dando la birra agli avversari più agguerriti curva dopo curva, gara dopo gara. Questo è il secondo titolo mondiale per Valentino, dopo il successo del '97 nella 125. Grazie al Racing Team Aprilia, grazie alle performance dello spumeggiante Valentino Rossi, il primo della classe (250!) e grazie a Nastro Azzurro, oggi più che mai la birra dal Gusto Vincente!
Vale più di tutti!
Nastro Azzurro
Il gusto vincente.

GENIUS ON THE TRACK AND MEDIA PHENOMENON OFF IT. VALENTINO'S ADVERTS ARE NEVER CONVENTIONAL. HE CUDDLES HIS BIKE, OR RESCUES THE BEAUTIFUL FERNANDA LESSA

H FEDERICA FONTANA IN THE MEDIASET STUDIOS, REVIEWING THE SPORTING YEAR. BELOW, IN A DANISH SAFETY CAMPAIGN AND PROMOTING THE HONDA CIVIC

ROSSI THE SAMURAI WITH JAPANESE ACTOR JOJI TOKORO, WITH HIS YAMAHA M1 IN THE BACKGROUND. BELOW, ROSSANO BRAZZI STYLE, WEARING HEADPHONES IN THE DEEJAY RADIO STUDIOS

WITH MICHELLE HUNZIKER

captivating as soon as anything really grabs his attention. Advertisers soon cottoned on to his uniqueness. After the fantastic title triumph of 2004, when the champion rode the inferior Yamaha to victory over his former employers, a market research survey 'discovered' that Valentino was the perfect representative for any product, far better than Michael Schumacher, or any other Italian sporting star. It was hardly rocket science; on the rare occasions that he has agreed to promote a product, he has been sensational.

Rossi is spectacular during races, and also afterwards. His unaffected style has slowly grown beyond the circle of traditional fans and conquered the world. It would be no surprise to see him in front of the cameras at the end of his racing career.

He looks the part too.

All celebrities, whether A or C-list, sportspeople or otherwise, try to meet him. Constructors and teams compete to bring celebrities to the paddock, to show them off. But whichever rider they declare themselves to be a fan of, the stars always end up trying to contact the lad from Tavullia.

It is no coincidence that this is particularly true of sports personalities. They know how difficult victory is to come by, but also how hard it is to manage what comes afterwards: the celebrations, the outbursts of joy, the interviews and the publicity.

Rossi has won everybody over with his celebratory post-race games, because he has found the correct balance between sport and showmanship. Even the great Michael Jordan wanted to meet him, in Valencia in 2004. It was the same fun-loving nature that led Valentino to test the Ferrari, the ultimate thrill.

ON TELEGATTI WITH GIORGIO PANARIELLO AND RAFFAELLA CARRÀ; WITH AN ARM AROUND AUSTRALIAN ATHLETE CATHY FREEMAN BY THE THAMES; WITH ALBERTO TOMBA ON THE STAGE AT SANREMO, DURIN

LA GAZZETTA FESTIVAL OF SPORT. VALENTINO IS ALWAYS SPONTANEOUS, EVEN WHEN PRESENTING STUDIO SPORT ON ITALIA 1.

AT THE SANREMO MUSIC FESTIVAL ROSSI LEADS PIPPO BAUDO ROUND THE STAGE. ABOVE, WI

LIST DAMIANO CUNEGO AND 'ACTRESS' CICCIOLINA. BELOW, WITH THE LEGENDARY JOHN SURTEES (ONLY WORLD CHAMPION ON BOTH 2 AND 4 WHEELS) AND WITH VASCO, THE OTHER WORLD-FAMOUS ROSSI

WITH LAPO ELKANN, THE FIAT GROUP'S MARKETING MANAGER

I'M A BIG FAN OF ROSSI'S. HIS IMAGE WOULD BE FANTASTIC FOR THE FIAT BRAND

LAPO ELKANN

VALE AND SCHUMI: 13 WORLD TITLES

VALENTINO WITH ROBERTO CARLOS AND RONALDO

It is no secret that Bernie Ecclestone would go to any lengths to have Vale rejuvenate his Formula One brand. Perhaps he thought of the idea himself, or maybe his wife Slaviza pointed it out to him, but when the couple visited the Portuguese Grand Prix in 2001 they had one major objective, which they accomplished: Mrs Ecclestone went home with Rossi's helmet as a trophy. Lapo Elkann's public adulation of the Italian rider is also well-known. His declarations could be seen as containing a touch of malice, given that the Fiat heir has replaced Valentino in the romantic affections of Martina Stella. This is one of the few times that a love story of Vale's has ended up in the public domain, and one of the very few in which he has been 'worsted'. It is Murphy's Law, and the

I GATECRASHED A FOOTBALLERS' PARTY TO HAVE DINNER WITH THEM. I WAS HUNGRY

VALE AND FOOTBALLER GATTUSO

WITH PIERLUIGI COLLINA: A RED CARD FOR QUARRELLING WITH BIAGGI?

PEAK
PERFORMANCE
GORE-TEX
GAULOISE
YAMAH
FACTORY RACIN

, WITH LUC ALPHAND AND DEBORAH COMPAGNONI. ABOVE, VALE WITH UMBERTO MASETTI, THE OTHER NO.46, AND GABRIEL BATISTUTA. BELOW, WITH BERNIE ECCLESTONE AND MAX PEZZALI

REPSOL
GAS
Milka
46
THE DOCTOR
MICHELIN
DIESEL
STOP

SI RIDING PIGGYBACK ON SKIER KRISTIAN GHEDINA. ABOVE, WITH GIACOMO AGOSTINI. BELOW, WITH PAOLO CEVOLI

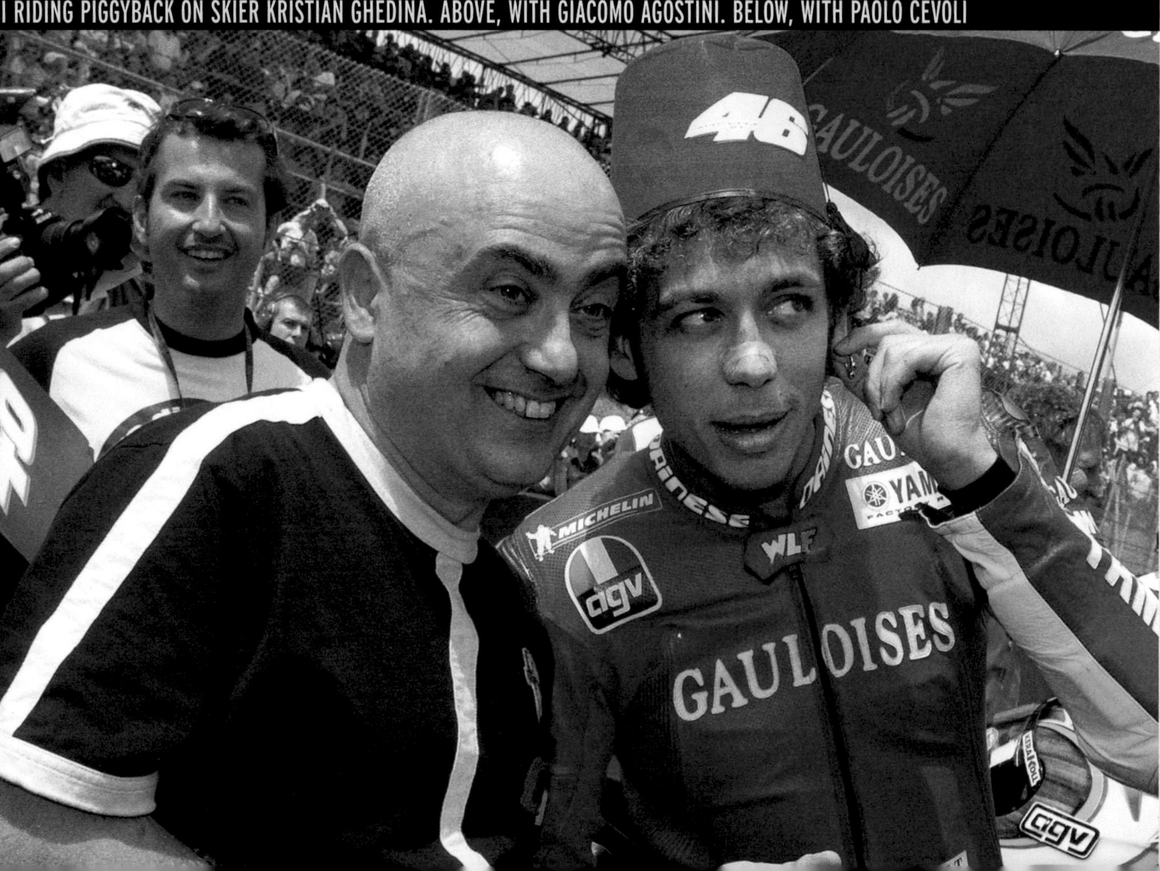

'revenge' of his enemy Max Biaggi, whom Rossi had accused of too many high-profile romances. Vale's first official girlfriend, Eliane, was a ballerina, but that was merely a coincidence. She was a girl from his area who happened to move in the same circles. Then came the celebrities, and like most top sportsmen, Vale has been linked with all kinds of models, cover girls etc, in an effort to fill the gossip columns. Once he was asked, 'How do you keep your privacy?' The answer was perfect: 'Simple, I go to bed early.' True, but only to a point. He forgot to add that he then goes out when everyone else is asleep . . .

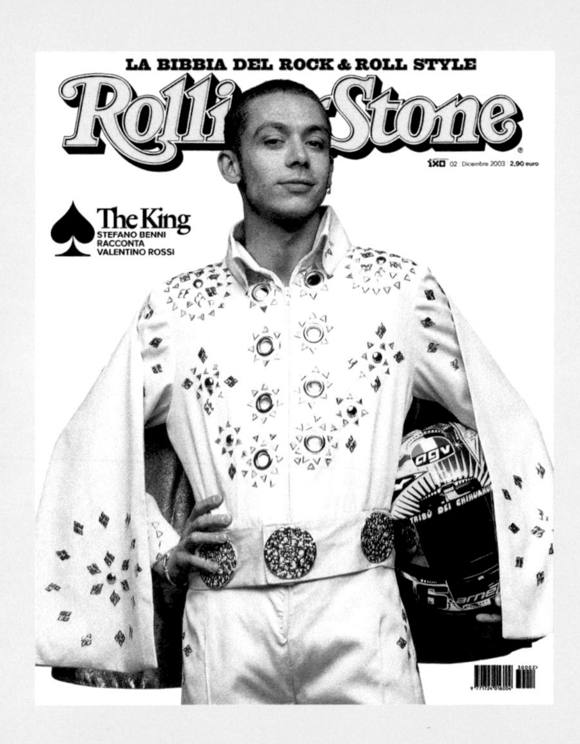

 VALENTINO IS FRONT PAGE NEWS. WHERE THE SIX-TIME WORLD CHAMPION IS INVOLVED, ART DIRECTORS TAKE THEIR CREATIVITY TO THE LIMIT. VALE NEVER DISAPPOINTS

'E, WITH MARTINA STELLA: A BRIEF BUT INTENSE LOVE STORY. BELOW, WITH ELIANE, HIS FIRST OFFICIAL GIRLFRIEND. SHE WAS A BALLERINA AND LIVED NEAR VALENTINO

ALL THE **COLOURS** OF THE SUPEROSSI

Valentino Rossi is only an unpredictable, creative maverick when in public. A bit like the sun and the moon on his helmet, in private Rossi is precise, meticulous and methodical to the extreme, both in racing and in life. To call it excessive would be an understatement, this borders on the compulsive. It would be limiting in many situations, but not when your job depends on your ability to coordinate a million and one different details to create the perfection more commonly attributed to a Stradivarius. In spite of his propensity for lateness – although he does not miss a second when it really counts – there are no half measures when Rossi is at work. It is in his nature to take pleasure from details, however insignificant.

DAINESE
REPSOL YPF
REPSOL
GAS
MANPOWER
NGK
HONDA
MICHELIN
agv
GO!!!!!!!
YAMAHA FACTORY RACING
MOTUL
KERAKOLL
YAMAHA
GREAT WHITE LONDON management

domino
DUNLOP
DAINESE
ろっしふみ
がんばって!

DUNLOP
DAINESE
polini
alpinestars
domino
LORIS BELLINI
Dyeing Machines
MEDIA RECORDS
aprilia

 FROM ROSSIFUMI IN 125CC TO THE DOCTOR IN 500CC-MOTOGP. THE NICKNAME MAY CHANGE BUT THE APPAREL SPONSOR, ITALIAN COMPANY DAINESE, REMAINS THE SAME. HIS LEATHERS ARE MULTICOLOU

RY THE MARKS OF A FEW (THANKFULLY RARE) FALLS AND BEAR THE UNMISTAKEABLE NUMBER 46, OFTEN ACCOMPANIED BY THE CHAMPIONS' NO.1 ON THE RIGHT SHOULDER

REPSOL
DAINESE
GAS
agv
HRC
HONDA RACING
REPSOL
GAS
GASJEANS.COM
HONDA
GREAT WHITE LONDON management
MICHELIN
MANPOWER
HONDA
REPSOL
DAINESE
REPSOL
GAS
GASJEANS.COM
HONDA
DAINESE
THE DOCTOR
REPSOL
DAINESE
GAS
agv
GAS
GASJEANS.COM
HONDA
GREAT WHITE LONDON management
MICHELIN
HONDA
REPSOL
DAINESE

REPSOL
GAS
GASJEANS.COM
HONDA
DAINESE
THE DOCTOR
HONDA
HONDA

MICHELIN
agv
DAINESE
DAINESE
GO!!!!!!!
YAMAHA
FACTORY RACING
MOTUL
GO!!!!!!!
GO!!!!!!!
MOTUL
KERAKOLL
YAMAHA
YAMAHA
GREAT
WHITE
LONDON
management
DAINESE
DAINESE

46
1
GO!!!!!!!
YAMAHA
DAINESE
THE DOCTOR

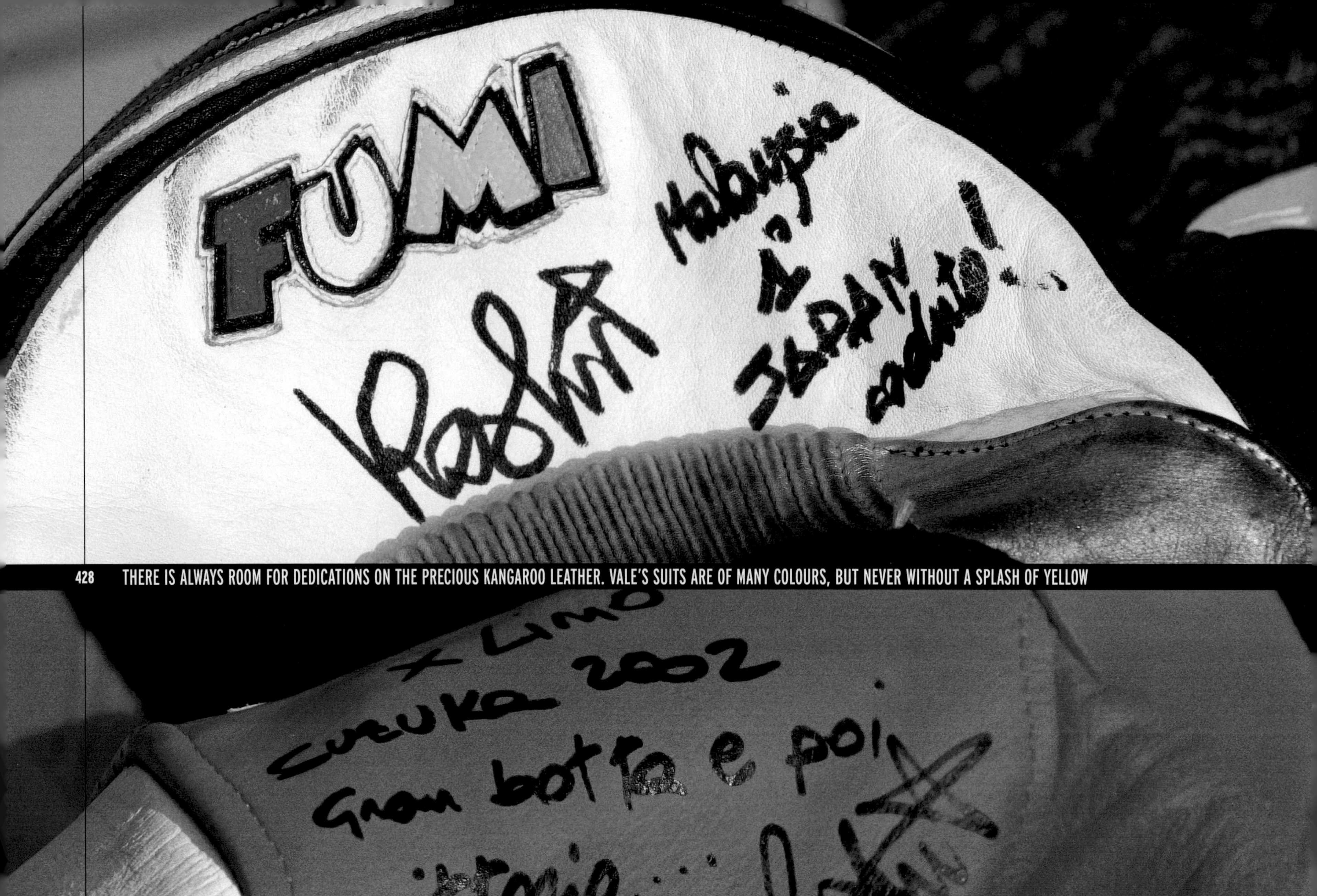

THERE IS ALWAYS ROOM FOR DEDICATIONS ON THE PRECIOUS KANGAROO LEATHER. VALE'S SUITS ARE OF MANY COLOURS, BUT NEVER WITHOUT A SPLASH OF YELLOW

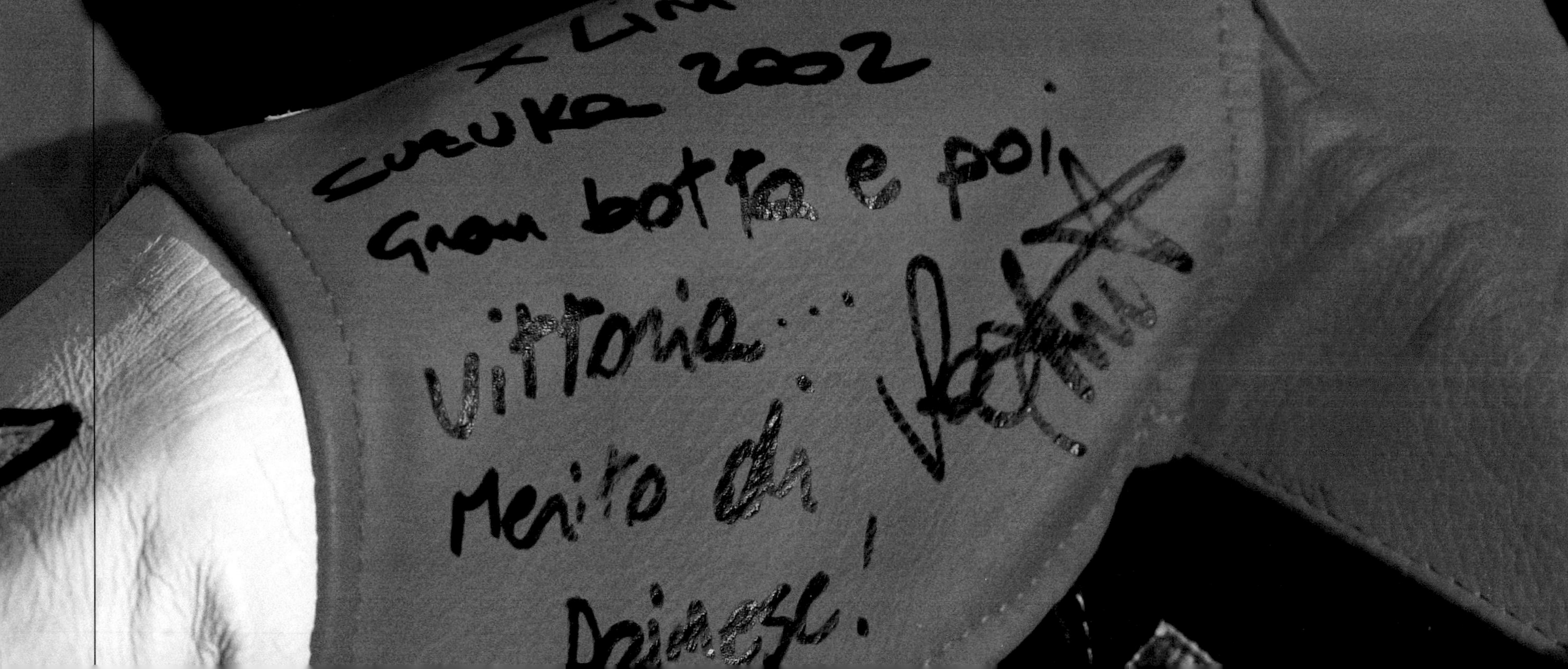

His suitcase, for example, is more like a boutique, with each item so carefully folded that it would drive even the most patient shop assistant crazy. Things are no different when he unpacks in hotel rooms, or in the motor home. Everything has its place, including his flip-flops, which are perfectly aligned with one another and on the floor.

Another fixture is the now threadbare Ninja turtle, the same one that was attached to his helmet with suckers during Valentino's first Minimoto races as a boy. It never leaves his side: 'I bought it at the Co-op with my mum and it's always been with me.' It is an inseparable friend: Vale has it tattooed on his stomach and also attaches it to his bike when he races.

GREAT
WHITE
LONDON
management
GAS
GASJEANS.COM
HONDA

THE LAST RACE OF 2003, VALENTINO CHOOSES A SPECIAL LOOK. AT VALENCIA HE RACES WITH A 70S-STYLE HONDA AND PRESENTS THE TOKYO CONSTRUCTOR WITH YET ANOTHER VICTORY

A SELECTION OF THE HELMETS WORN BY ROSSI IN THE WORLD CHAMPIONSHIP: 'I'VE HAD THE SUN AND THE MOON ON MY LIDS SINCE I FIRST STARTED RACING. I LIKE THE WAY THEY LOOK AND TH

RESENT ME UP TO A POINT. DAY AND NIGHT, GOOD AND BAD, BEAUTY AND BEAST, ANGEL AND DEVIL – THE CHARACTERISTICS EVERY GOOD RIDER NEEDS'

IN VALENTINO'S HELMET COLLECTION ARE SOME GENUINE JEWELS, LIKE THE GOLD HELMETS (ABOVE LEFT) HIS SPONSOR HAS HAD MADE FOR HIM BY MASTER GOLDSMITHS SINCE 2002. 5 KILOS OF SOLID

D PLUS DIAMONDS AND ONYX, WORTH ABOUT 180,000 EUROS. 'I PUT THEM IN THE BANK, SO WHEN MY MONEY RUNS OUT I'LL HAVE SOMETHING TO FALL BACK ON'

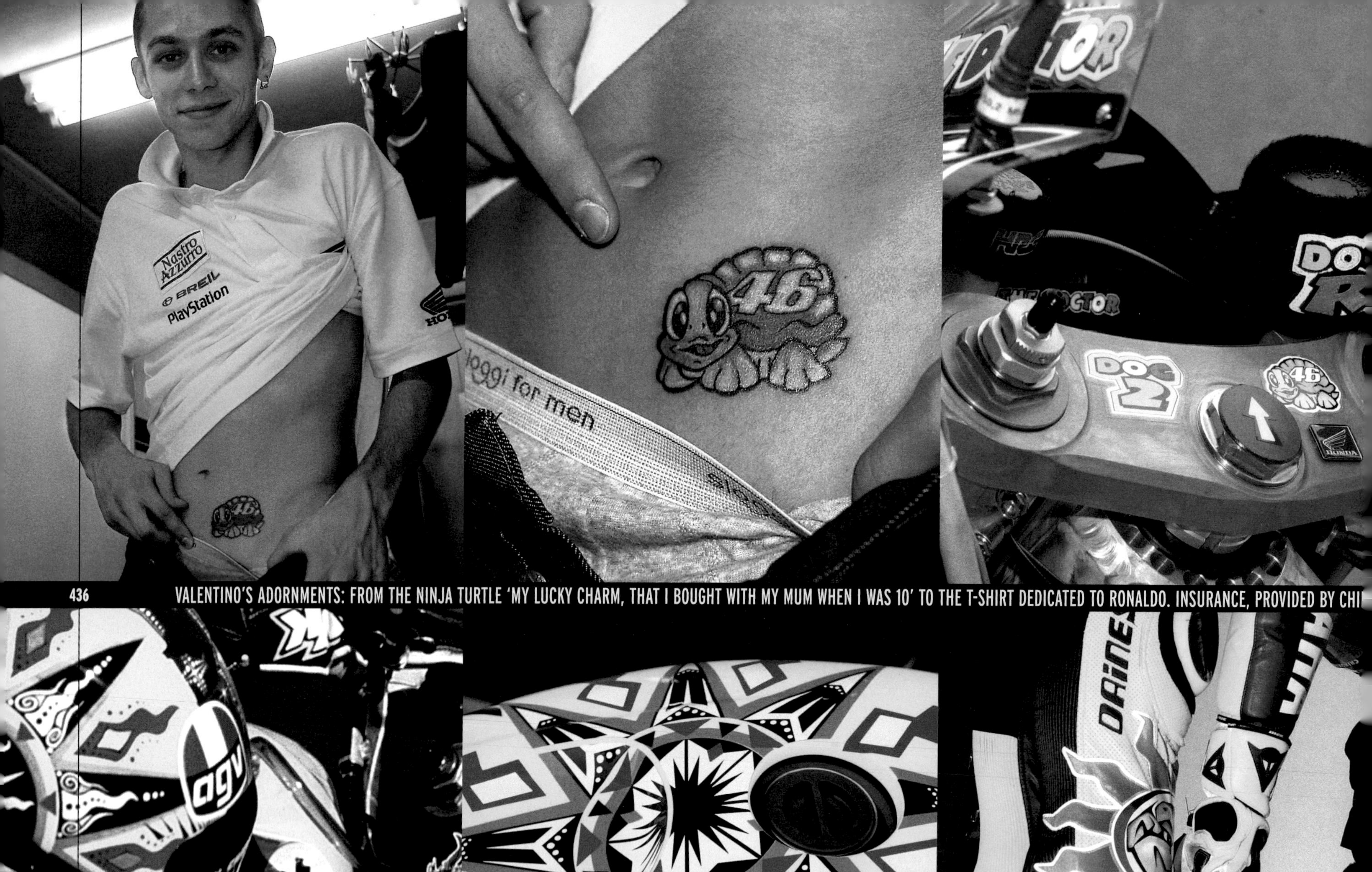

VALENTINO'S ADORNMENTS: FROM THE NINJA TURTLE 'MY LUCKY CHARM, THAT I BOUGHT WITH MY MUM WHEN I WAS 10' TO THE T-SHIRT DEDICATED TO RONALDO. INSURANCE, PROVIDED BY CHI

JEREMY BURGESS ASSICURAZIONI ALDGATE

CONTRASSEGNO DI ASSICURAZIONE

TARGA VEICOLO O DATI NATANTE

VR 46

TIPO DEL VEICOLO

MOTORETTA CV. 230 più o meno

SCADENZA PERIODO ASSICURATIVO	GIORNO	MESE	ANNO
	01	11	2002

R4603

JEREMY BURGESS ASSICURAZIONI

HANIC JEREMY BURGESS, IS MANDATORY. THE LATEST PENCHANT IS FOR A FABRIC RING. BEARING THE NO.46 OF COURSE

 VARIOUS VERSIONS OF THE DOCTOR, VALENTINIK AND GUIDO, THE EMBLEMS THAT ACCOMPANY ALL VALE'S EXPLOITS. THERE IS NO LACK OF CREATIVITY. THE BULLDOG CHANGES ITS ATTIRE TO MATCH THE FAIR

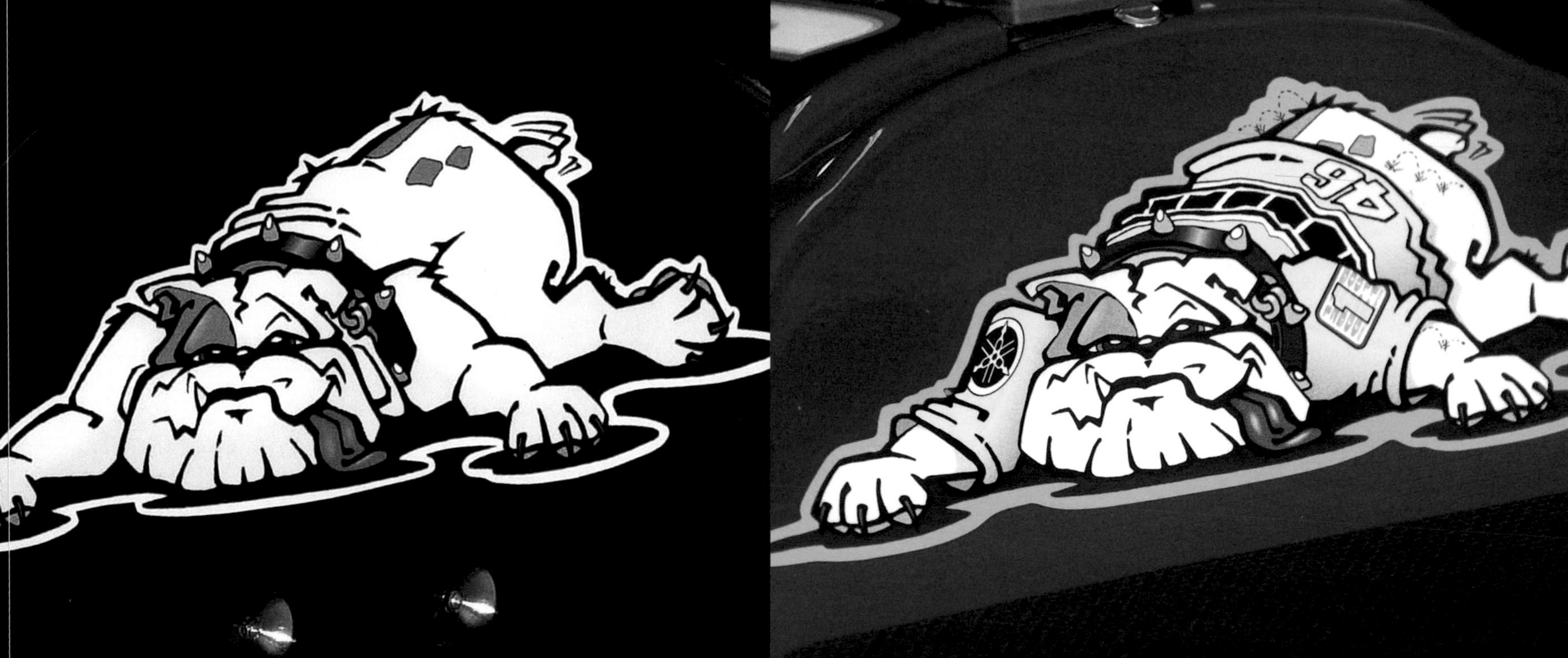

IGN; AN EXTRA SPLASH OF COLOUR THAT MAKES THE BIKES UNIQUE. WHETHER HE'S RIDING FOR HONDA OR YAMAHA, VALENTINO'S HALLMARKS REMAIN THE SAME

 WITH A BAR CODE REPLACING AN ALCOHOL SPONSOR, OR FLOWER POWER: TWO OF VALENTINO'S BIKE'S 'COSTUMES'. THE ITALIAN'S TALENT KNOWS NO BOUNDS: IT EVEN INSPIRED A DUTCH GROWER,

DUCED A ROSE CALLED VALENTINO ROSSI – YELLOW OF COURSE, LIKE THE SEVEN-TIME WORLD CHAMPION'S NUMBER 46

Valentino has been writing efficiency lists in his beautiful, neat handwriting since he was a boy. On them, he would set out mainly, but not exclusively, what he needed to do on the bike. The area reserved for him in the pits is, and has always been, a perfect reflection of the champion's temperament. It contains a foam mat he thinks he found or received as a gift, on which his cap and gloves are always laid out in exactly the same position. There are also earplugs, essential on today's ultra-noisy MotoGP bikes and the device Rossi uses to prevent tooth-grinding, an unconscious habit that many riders have. This tiny device – and here we enter the realms of obsession – is labelled with a small coloured 'VR' sticker.

A fixation with designs and logos is Valentino's trademark. Ever since he first started out he has been decorating his world and the entire World Championship with a series of creative stunts. But make no mistake, this is no game – more like a full-time job!

The stickers may seem strange to most people, who would place the logo 'roughly' there. But getting to within centimetres of the right place is not enough: here we are talking millimetres. The text is moved about (with the aid of an industrial strength blow dryer) until the perfect placement is found. You can imagine the work involved, especially when you have to take the contours of a motorcycle into account as well . . .

But stickers are lively. They send out a message and are fun. During Rossi's ten years as a racer, we have seen all sorts, thanks also to the creative genius of Aldo Drudi, a friend of his father Graziano's, who has been infected with the champion's inventiveness. Nothing illustrates the masterful absurdity behind their game better than the tax and insurance label, identical to that on a road bike, which was first conceived of during Vale's days in 250cc. It contains all the required information: power of the 'motor vehicle' (approximate, because certain information cannot be made public), the Tavullia office which supposedly issued the policy, and the insurer, who is the chief mechanic. It used to be Rossano Brazzi until Valentino graduated to the half-litre championship, when the Australian Jeremy Burgess took his place.

There are, however, infinite examples of Rossi's resourcefulness ranging from his encouragement to the legendary Brazilian Ronaldo when he injured his knee, to the multicoloured graffiti and distinctive livery he uses for special occasions. There is also Guido, the bulldog, on the saddle of

VALENTINO'S BIKES MAY CHANGE, BUT THE RITUALS REMAIN THE SAME. PUTTING IN THE EARPLUGS, STRETCHING AT THE EXIT TO THE PITS, CROUCHING DOWN BY THE BIKE; THESE ARE ALL GESTURES THAT

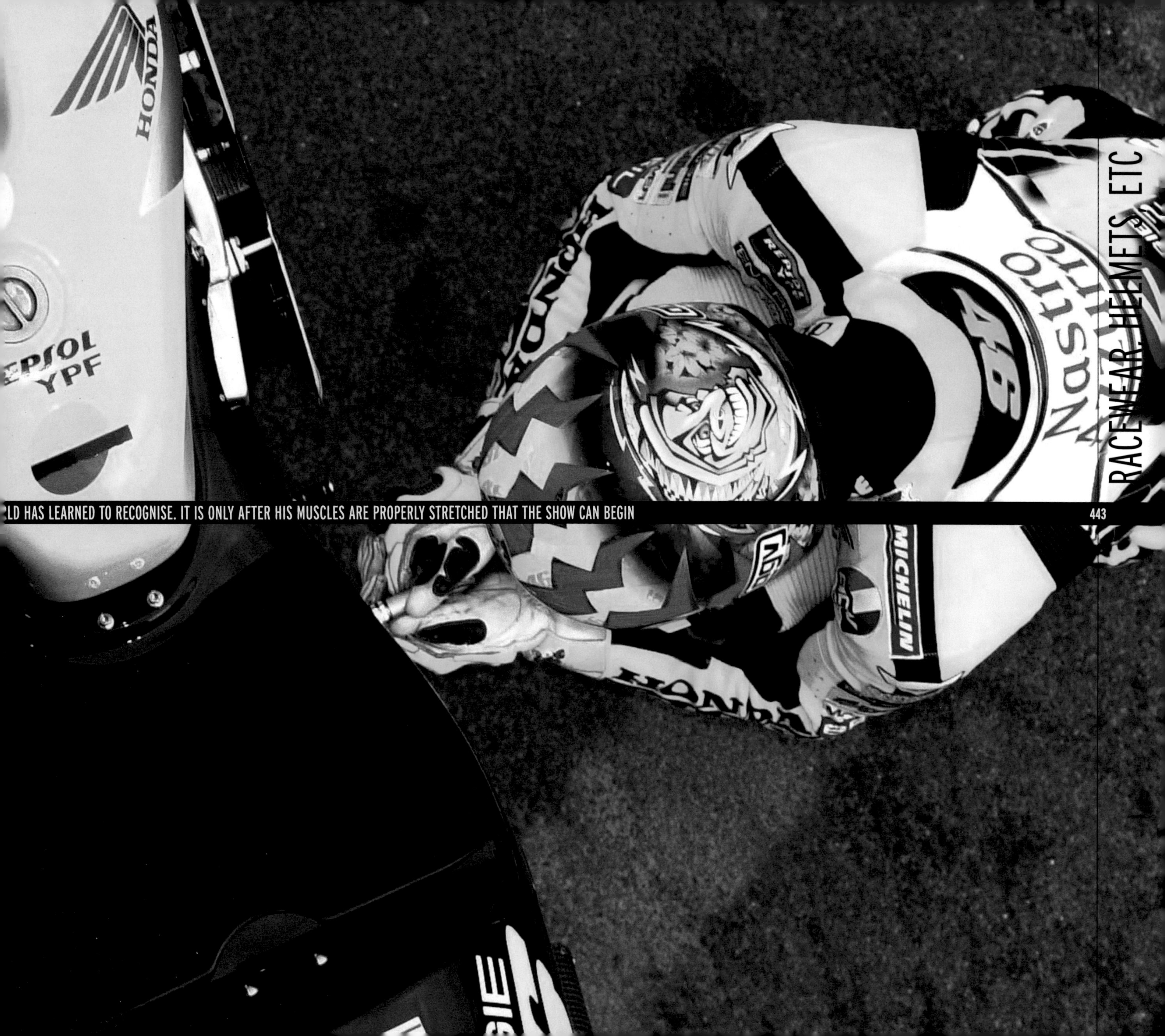

LD HAS LEARNED TO RECOGNISE. IT IS ONLY AFTER HIS MUSCLES ARE PROPERLY STRETCHED THAT THE SHOW CAN BEGIN

his bike, who appeared dressed jailbird-style after the post-victory convict sketch at Brno in 2003. There was even a fake joystick on the tank when Valentino was being sponsored by PlayStation.

As well as the stickers, there are the T-shirts, particularly for special occasions such as World Championship victories, or one-off situations, like the almost-forgotten comparison with a Fiat 500 for winter testing in 2000, the year he moved up into the premier class.

His helmets are another important way in which Vale expresses himself. The sun and moon are ever-present, but there are infinite variations. In addition, many different versions of the Italian flag have been used. There are two particularly memorable helmets: the old-style 'Tricolore' that Rossi wore at Mugello in 2002, in imitation of his father, and the Dash container that made an appearance in testing during the winter of 2004-05, to 'clean the dirt out of the World Championship'. The rider's other habits have become rituals, known to fans around the world. They originated as pre-race muscle stretches, because a thorough warm-up is essential for a rider enclosed in the protective leather all-in-one suit. First he stretches, with his feet lined up with the very edge of the pit area, then crouches down by the bike in a 'foetal' position, clasping his motorcycle's right-hand footrest in order to become 'one' with the machine. Then finally, he stands up straight on the footrests while going down the pit lane, adjusting his underpants and other clothing for the greatest possible comfort. Now it has all simply become traditional; these are the details that make up the legend.

HE ADJUSTS HIS LEATHERS BEFORE THE RACE. ROSSI SWINGS HIS RIGHT LEG OVER THE TANK TO DISMOUNT (NEXT PAGE)

46
REPSOL
HONDA
GAS
agv
Repsol Honda
dainese
HRC
BLUE JEANS

STANDING ON THE YAMAHA M1 AS HE CROSSES THE FINISHING LINE. ON THE RIGHT IS HIS PERSONALISED SIGN: THE DOCTOR

-START THE POST-RACE EXTRAVAGANZA

Published by Yellow Jersey Press 2006

1 2 3 4 5 6 7 8 9 10

First published as *TuttoVale* in Italy in 2005 by Rizzoli Libri Illustrati

First published in Great Britain in 2006 by Yellow Jersey Press

Yellow Jersey Press
Random House, 20 Vauxhall Bridge Road,
London SW1V 2SA

Random House Australia (Pty) Limited
20 Alfred Street, Milsons Point, Sydney,
New South Wales 2061, Australia

Random House New Zealand Limited
18 Poland Road, Glenfield,
Auckland 10, New Zealand

Random House (Pty) Limited
Isle of Houghton, Corner of Boundary Road
& Carse O'Gowrie,
Houghton, 2198, South Africa

Random House Publishers India Private Limited
301 World Trade Tower,
Hotel Intercontinental Grand Complex,
Barakhamba Lane, New Delhi 110 001, India

The Random House Group Limited Reg. No. 954009
www.randomhouse.co.uk

A CIP catalogue record for this book is available from the British Library

ISBN 9780224080118 (From Jan 07)
ISBN 0224080113

Papers used by Random House are natural, recyclable products made from wood grown in sustainable forests. The manufacturing processes conform to the environmental regulations of the country of origin

Printed and bound in Germany by
Appl Druck, Wemding